1992

RESEARCH WITH HISPANIC POPULATIONS

Applied Social Research Methods Series
Volume 23

APPLIED SOCIAL RESEARCH
METHODS SERIES

Series Editors:
LEONARD BICKMAN, Peabody College, Vanderbilt University, Nashville
DEBRA J. ROG, Vanderbilt University, Washington, DC

RESEARCH WITH HISPANIC POPULATIONS

Gerardo Marín
Barbara VanOss Marín

Applied Social Research Methods Series
Volume 23

SAGE PUBLICATIONS
The International Professional Publishers
Newbury Park   London   New Delhi

Para nuestros hijos, Melisa Ann Marín y Andrés Daniel Marín

For information address:

SAGE Publications, Inc.
2455 Teller Road
Newbury Park, California 91320

SAGE Publications Ltd.
6 Bonhill Street
London EC2A 4PU
United Kingdom

SAGE Publications India Pvt. Ltd.
M-32 Market
Greater Kailash I
New Delhi 110 048 India

Printed in the United States of America

Library of Congress Cataloging-in-Publication Data

Marín, Gerardo.
    Research with Hispanic populations / Gerardo Marín and Barbara VanOss
Marín.
        p.   cm. — (Applied social research methods series: v. 23)
    Includes bibliographical references and index.
    ISBN 0-8039-3720-2 (c). — ISBN 0-8039-3721-0 (p)
    1. Hispanic Americans—Research—Methodology.   I. Marín, Barbara
VanOss.   II. Title.   III. Series.
E184.S75M38   1991
973'.0468—dc20   90-26197
                                                                                  CIP

FIRST PRINTING, 1991

Sage Production Editor: Michelle R. Starika

Contents

Preface and Acknowledgments

During the first days of 1980, the mass media and social scientists alike proclaimed the 1980s the "Decade of the Hispanic," due in part to Hispanics' significant impact on the demography of the United States. Indeed, the 1980 census would show that the number of Hispanics residing in the country had grown by 265% between 1950 and 1980. This renewed interest in Hispanics during the 1980s brought an understanding of the historic role played by Hispanics since the times of the European colonization of the Americas as well as small glimpses of an ethnic group endowed with important cultural strengths, aware of its problems and of its potential political strength.

As the 1990s begin, the Hispanic population continues to play an important role in the life of the nation in a number of ways. First, the number of Hispanics can be expected to continue to increase (an average of 4.3% per year according to Bureau of the Census estimates). Second, the role of Hispanics in the national life should become more salient: The 1980s saw a Hispanic astronaut, two cabinet positions filled by Hispanics in the Bush administration, well-known Hispanic figures in the entertainment world (such as Gloria Estefan and Charlie Sheen), and prominent Hispanics in the world of science, business, and industry. Third, we can expect a renewed awareness of the important problems experienced by Hispanics during the last few years such as prejudice, discrimination, and institutional racism; low academic achievement; serious health problems; lack of access to public services; poor housing; and unemployment and underemployment. Culturally appropriate research is needed in identifying and solving these problems that affect Hispanics. For example, future studies should be able to help us better understand and prevent the scandously high rate of Hispanic adolescents who never finish high school (35.7%), a rate that is almost triple that of Whites and double that of Blacks. Better research is also needed to address the high rate of infection with the Human Immunodeficency Virus (HIV) and of individuals with AIDS (Acquired Immune Deficiency Syndrome) among Hispanics—twice the proportion of Hispanics in the population. In addition, a wide range of other areas are in need of culturally sensitive research with Hispanics. These include a better understanding of such large and important components of group life as issues of employment, political power, career development, and economic status as well as a better understanding of Hispanic cultural characteristics, basic values, attitudes, expectancies, and social behaviors.

The number of studies with Hispanics in the social and behavioral sciences increased a thousandfold during the 1980s. Unfortunately, many researchers naively assumed that the methods and research approaches that were useful with non-Hispanic Whites could also be utilized with Hispanics. In general, little attention was paid to the proper way of translating instruments, the development of culturally appropriate research procedures, or the measurement of significant moderating variables such as acculturation, language preference, and generation.

The idea for this book was born from our contacts with colleagues and from finding in the scientific literature that important issues were being addressed by researchers with a methodology so faulty that it rendered the results uninterpretable or misleading. We hoped that by compiling in one place the experiences of various researchers in conducting studies with Hispanics, future investigators would be able to address properly the methodological limitations that have plagued so much of the early writings on Hispanics.

In writing this book we have tried to include the experiences and suggestions of a large number of authors who have conducted research with Hispanics in the last few years. In some cases we have emphasized one solution over the other possibilities based on our experiences over the last few years in which we have studied well over 14,000 Hispanics. Because this is a rapidly developing area, the reader should keep in mind that new approaches may be developed in the next few years that make some of our suggestions obsolete. As a matter of fact, we hope that by writing this book, we will motivate methodologists to produce better and more creative solutions to some of the problems we discuss here.

We have dedicated this book to our children, Melisa Ann and Andrés Daniel, in the hope that as members of a new Hispanic generation they will reap the benefits of improved research methodologies. As intellectual children of Kurt Lewin, we feel that there is little that is more practical that a good theory, and good theory must depend on good research. We hope that students and researchers inexperienced with

Hispanics will find in this book solutions to important methodological problems that will lead them to design and conduct better studies.

As with any book, this one has benefited from the contributions of a number of individuals. First, of course, are the many researchers who in the past expressed concern about the limitations of traditional research methodologies. Their names are many, but we hope that by including some of their research findings and ideas in the text of the book we are acknowledging our intellectual debt to them. We have also learned much from our interactions with our research colleagues. They are also many—but one, Harry C. Triandis, deserves special mention here for shaping our perspectives on the difficulties encountered when studying a group's culture.

We wish to acknowledge the incisive criticisms and excellent suggestions provided by those individuals who reviewed initial drafts of the book: Raymond J. Gamba; Rolando Juarez, M.A.; Ricardo Muñoz, Ph.D.; Eliseo J. Pérez-Stable, M.D.; Samuel Posner; and, Harry C. Triandis, Ph.D. Their comments made this book more readable and useful to future readers and scholars.

Significant proportions of our research experiences mentioned in this book were gathered as we participated in a number of research projects funded by various agencies. In particular we wish to acknowledge the help provided by the following: Contract N00014-80-C-0407 from the Office of Naval Research (H. C. Triandis, Principal Investigator); grant CA 39260 from the National Cancer Institute (E. J. Pérez-Stable, B. Marín, & G. Marín, Principal Investigators); grant AA08545 from the National Institute on Alcohol Abuse and Alcoholism (G. Marín, Principal Investigator); grant DA04928 from the National Institute on Drug Abuse; and grant MH46777 from the National Institute of Mental Health (B. Marín, Principal Investigator). The preparation of this book was partially supported by the last four grants and by a sabbatical leave from the University of San Francisco to one of us (G. M.).

Gerardo Marín
Barbara VanOss Marín

1

Hispanics:
Who Are They?

The purpose of this first chapter is to present a concise overview of the demography, history, and culture of Hispanics in the United States. The information presented here is meant to provide a backdrop to the issues discussed in the following chapters by making salient some basic characteristics of Hispanics. These important aspects of the Hispanic experience need to be considered whenever research is planned with members of this ethnic group. Because it is difficult to address completely these issues within the page limitations of the chapter, the publications referenced throughout the text should be consulted in order to obtain a more comprehensive understanding of Hispanics in the United States.

WHO IS A HISPANIC?

The term "Hispanic" is a label of convenience utilized to refer to those individuals who reside in the United States and who were born in or trace the background of their families to one of the Spanish-speaking Latin American nations or to Spain. It should be noted here that the label "Hispanic" is not universally accepted by its referents, and alternative labels (discussed in Chapter 2) have been suggested in the past.

The label "Hispanic" is used by government institutions (e.g., the Bureau of the Census) and the media as well as by health care, social, and behavioral scientists to refer to individuals that have very disparate migrational and sociodemographic characteristics. Nevertheless, members of this group share some common basic cultural values that, as explained below, make them members of a clearly identifiable group. Contrary to the assumptions of some individuals, cultural values—not demographic characteristics—help Hispanics self-identify as members of one same ethnic group. It is clear, for example, that not all Hispanics share a common language (Spanish) and religious faith (Roman Catholicism), although a majority of them speak Spanish and are Roman

1

Catholic. The significance ascribed to values such as familialism (the importance of relatives as referents and as providers of emotional support) and to social scripts such as "*simpatía*" (the preference for positive interpersonal interactions), are characteristics shared by most Hispanics independent of their national background, birthplace, dominant language, or any other sociodemographic characteristic.

As with any label of convenience utilized in demographic research or even in much of the social and behavioral sciences, the label "Hispanic," like the labels "Black," "White Anglo-Saxon Protestant," or "Irish-American," implies commonalities despite some significant differences among its referents. For example, Rosa, a descendent of Spanish settlers who resides in New Mexico and no longer speaks Spanish, should be considered as Hispanic as José, an undocumented Nicaraguan who has just arrived in the United States. What unites these two individuals is the common cultural values that remain strong and personally significant across generations and that may lead both Rosa and José to think of themselves as sharing "something" that they do not share with non-Hispanic residents of the United States.

The term "Hispanic" is used by the Bureau of the Census as an ethnic label (see Chapter 2) and not to denote a race because Hispanics belong to all of the human races (White as well as Black, Asian, and indigenous Native American). As a matter of fact, most Hispanics are racially mixed, including combinations of European White, African Black, and American Indian.

As an ethnic label, the work "Hispanic" goes beyond the race and national origin of its referents to denote a group of individuals who share important cultural values. In this sense, ethnicity is the collection of group-specific behaviors that are mediated by those shared social values that are characteristic of a given group (Tajfel & Turner, 1979). This is an important concern since many researchers still make the mistake of using "Hispanic" as a racial label and not as the name of an ethnic group. While it may be appropriate to compare responses or behaviors of African-Americans and Hispanics or of Hispanics and non-Hispanic Whites, researchers should not assume that these labels are necessarily mutually exclusive. It is possible for an individual to be ethnically Hispanic and racially Black or White at the same time. In fact, in the 1980 Bureau of the Census data about 3% of Hispanics reported being Black. Lack of understanding of the meaning of ethnicity and carelessness in the design of research projects have contributed to the misconception that Hispanics are a race different from Whites and Blacks.

Research with Hispanics as an ethnic group follows significant traditions in the social sciences for studying other ethnic groups in the United States such as the Polish (Thomas & Znaniecki, 1918), Jews (Potok, 1978), Greek-Americans (Moskos, 1980), Irish-Americans (Fellows, 1979; Maguire, 1969), and Asian-Americans (Knoll, 1982). These studies have looked at the respective ethnicities and their process of acculturation as well as maintenance of their ethno-specific values, attitudes, and behaviors. Most of these studies of ethnic groups have faced methodological problems similar to those covered in this book although there are specific issues (mentioned in other chapters) that researchers need to address when working with Hispanics.

GENERAL DEMOGRAPHIC CHARACTERISTICS OF HISPANICS

The 1980 census showed that there were 14.6 million Hispanics residing in the United States. This means that approximately 6.4% of the total population of the country was Hispanic at that time (Bureau of the Census, 1982) while 11.8% was Black, and 2.4% was Asian, Pacific Islanders, and Native Americans.

The 1980 census figures also showed that the proportion of Hispanics in the U.S. population is rapidly increasing. In the 30 years between the 1950 and the 1980 census, Hispanics increased by about 265% compared with a little less than 50% for the total population of the country in the same time period (Davis, Haub, & Willette, 1983). The 1988 Current Population Survey conducted by the Bureau of the Census estimated that there were 19.4 million Hispanics residing in the United States (8.1% of the total population). This new figure represents an increase in the total Hispanic population of 34.4% in the eight years since the 1980 census. As a comparison, the total population of the country was estimated in 1988 to have increased 8.4% since the 1980 census (Bureau of the Census, 1988). Predictions of the growth of the Hispanic population indicate that by the year 2020 there will be over 47 million Hispanics in the United States, representing 15% of the total population and thus becoming the nation's largest minority group (Davis et al., 1983). A more recent estimation by the Bureau of the Census (1986) suggests that if Hispanic immigration and fertility remain relatively high with low mortality, the Hispanic population of the country by the year 2020 would reach 54.3 million. These same

estimates suggest that by the year 2080, Hispanics would have increased to 140.7 million compared with 15.8 million in 1982.

U.S. Hispanics or their families come from one of the 19 Spanish-
speaking countries in the Americas, from Puerto Rico (a commonwealth
of the United States), or from Spain. Some countries have contributed
disproportionately to the pool of initial Hispanic immigrants to the
United States. The 1980 census showed that 59.8% of Hispanics were
of Mexican descent, while 13.8% traced their family background to
Puerto Rico and 5.5% to Cuba; and 20.9% were labeled "Other Hispanics," which includes those whose families came from any of the other
Latin American countries or from Spain (Bureau of the Census, 1982).
The 1988 estimates by the Bureau of the Census showed a significant
increase in the proportion of those of Mexican background: 62.3% of
the Hispanic population were of Mexican origin in 1988, 12.7% Puerto
Rican, 5.3% Cuban, and 19.6% were "Other Hispanics" (Bureau of the
Census, 1988).

Based on the migratory experiences of the last few years it can be
expected that the 1990 census will again show a marked increase in
the number of Hispanics residing in the United States. This change will
be due to a relatively heavy influx of immigrants from some Central
American countries (e.g., El Salvador, Guatemala, Nicaragua, Honduras), high fertility rates (25.5 per 1,000 compared to 14.7 per 1,000 for
non-Hispanics), as well as to the more frequent migrations motivated
by family reunification, financial improvement, and access to better
educational opportunities. It can also be expected that once the 1990
census figures are released, the majority of Hispanics will continue to
be of Mexican origin followed by a significant proportion who trace
their background to Central and South America. Political instability
and economic difficulties of Central and South American countries as
well as interest in family reunification are probably the key reasons for
these increases in migration to the United States.

While Hispanics can be found in all 50 states and in all territories of
the United States, the majority reside in four states: California (31.1%),
Texas (20.4%), New York (11.4%), and Florida (5.9%; Bureau of the
Census, 1982). These figures reflect migration patterns to border states
and to areas where air travel was easy and economical (as in the case
of Puerto Rican migration to New York). Nevertheless, it should be
kept in mind that large numbers of Hispanics can also be found outside
these four states. For example, according to the 1980 census, 6 of the
top 20 cities in the number of Hispanics are not part of the four states

with the largest concentrations of Hispanics: Chicago, Albuquerque, Phoenix, Denver, Philadelphia, and Tucson.

According to a recent report by the Bureau of the Census (1989), the majority of the Hispanic population (87%) lives in metropolitan areas; compared with three-quarters of the general population of the country. A substantial number of cities have a significant proportion of Hispanics. For example, 82.9% of the population of McAllen, Texas, is Hispanic, while 67.5% of El Paso, Texas, is Hispanic. Other cities with large proportions of Hispanics are San Antonio (46.5%), Miami (28.3%), Los Angeles (28.3%), San Diego (16.6%), Houston (16.7%), Phoenix (13.8%), New York (13.2%), and San Francisco (13.2%; Bureau of the Census, 1989).

The geographic distribution of the various Hispanic subgroups varies markedly. The majority (61%) of Puerto Ricans live in the New York and New Jersey areas. Most Mexican-Americans live in the Southwestern states (Arizona, California, Colorado, New Mexico, Texas) while the majority of Cuban-Americans (58%) reside in Florida. Nevertheless, it is becoming increasingly difficult to characterize a given city as being influenced by one particular Hispanic subgroup. New York City, for example, has large numbers of Dominicans and Colombians together with a sizable population of Puerto Ricans. Dade County in Florida, while predominantly Cuban, has had a recent influx of Nicaraguans and Colombians; and San Francisco now has more Central Americans than Mexican-Americans (*Hispanic Almanac,* 1984).

A perusal of the census results show that Hispanics as a group have some sociodemographic characteristics that differentiate them from other ethnic or racial groups. These characteristics, summarized below, have been derived from a number of reports issued by the Bureau of the Census (e.g., 1982, 1988, 1989) and from analyses of those results (*Hispanic Almanac,* 1984; Davis et al., 1983). These findings should be kept in mind whenever research involving Hispanics is planned since they could determine the expected characteristics of the sample, the type of instrumentation needed, the ease with which a sample can be accessed, and the generalizability of certain findings. As is true for any statistical report that relies on averages of a group, the data reported below obscure the fact that there is variability among Hispanics. Nevertheless, statistical averages allow for a rapid overview of a group's sociodemographic characteristics.

In general, Hispanics in the United States share the following characteristics:

Place of residence. Hispanics are primarily residents of urban or metropolitan areas; 87% live in Standard Metropolitan Areas as defined by the Bureau of the Census and approximately half of all Hispanics live in the central areas of large cities.

Age. As a group, Hispanics are very young. The median age in 1988 was 25.5 years compared with 32.2 years for the country as a whole. Approximately 11% of Hispanics were 5 years old or younger in 1988 compared with 8% of the total population.

Head of household. In 1982, a large proportion of Hispanic households (21.5%) were headed by a woman, compared with 15% of non-Hispanic households.

Educational level. According to 1980 figures, the average educational level of Hispanics is lower than that of the country as a whole. Of those Hispanics who are at least 25 years old, only 44% have completed 12 years of formal education, compared with 68% of non-Hispanics. Approximately 20% of Hispanics have obtained some college training, compared with 32% of the nation's residents. A significant proportion of Hispanics 25 years and older (17.6%) have had fewer than 5 years of formal education, compared with 12.7% of non-Hispanic Whites and 9.6% of Blacks.

Income. Median income of Hispanics is lower than that of non-Hispanics. In 1987, the median income for Hispanic families was $20,306, compared with $31,610 for all non-Hispanic families. That same year approximately 25.8% of Hispanic families had incomes below the poverty line, compared with 11% for the population as a whole.

Occupational status. In general, Hispanics are clustered in blue-collar and semi-skilled jobs (58%), and a significant proportion are unemployed—8.5% in 1982 compared with 5.8% of non-Hispanics.

Language preference. The majority of Hispanics speak Spanish at home (63%) and a significant proportion speak little or no English (25%).

As mentioned above, these statistics are for all Hispanics residing in the United States. Subgroup differences that have been ignored in this summary can in some cases be quite important. For example, in 1988, the median age of all Hispanics was 25.5 years. Mexican-Americans and Puerto Ricans had lower median ages (23.9 and 24.9 years, respectively) while Cuban-Americans had a much higher median age (38.7 years). Central and South Americans were somewhere in between (27.6 years). Comparable subgroup difference are also found in the other sociodemographic characteristics mentioned above.

Researchers should consult the latest reports from the Bureau of the Census in order to better understand the population to be studied. The Bureau of the Census maintains a Hispanic Office where information on available reports and sources of data can be obtained.

HISTORICAL BACKGROUND

Hispanics in the United States are not necessarily newcomers. As early as 1513 there were Spanish explorers and settlers in what is now the continental United States. Additional settlements and towns were established within the next few decades in what is now Florida, Texas, California, New Mexico, and Colorado. Spaniards played a significant role in the founding of such major contemporary cities as San Antonio, El Paso, Los Angeles, San Francisco, Tucson, and San Diego (Acosta-Belén, 1988).

Early in the nineteenth century, Spain gave up possession of Louisiana to the French and sold Florida to the United States. Also during the beginning of the nineteenth century, settlements of non-Hispanics were being established in California and in Texas, turning those areas into multicultural enclaves. These non-Hispanics produced important changes in the political and cultural life of those territories, and in 1836 non-Hispanic settlers in Texas declared independence from Mexico. A few years later, in 1846, war broke out between Mexico and the United States. The peace treaty signed in 1848 forced Mexico to give up almost half of its territory, most of which is now Arizona, California, Colorado, Kansas, Nevada, New Mexico, Oklahoma, Utah, and Wyoming.

The massive incorporation of Hispanic groups into the continental United States continued in 1898, when the United States took possession of Cuba, Puerto Rico, Hawaii, Guam, and the Philippines as part of the Spanish-American war. Cuba was granted independence in 1902 while Puerto Rico became a commonwealth of the United States in 1952. The result of these wars and treaties was the annexation of significant stretches of land with large numbers of Hispanics. More recent social and political events in various Latin American countries have been responsible for the migration of large numbers of Latin Americans to the United States, a process that has not necessarily slowed down.

Mexican-Americans

Those individuals of Spanish and Mexican descent who lived in the territories annexed at the time of the 1848 peace treaty with Mexico were given a choice of citizenship. Many of those who remained in the United States, particularly in New Mexico, continued to intermarry with non-Hispanics and with Native Americans and became known as "Hispanos." These early settlers of the Southwest formed the first group of Mexican-Americans and were the ancestors of current fourth- and fifth-generation Hispanics who reside primarily in the southwestern United States. They, like American Indians, had settled the land before it became part of the United States.

The largest increase in the number of Mexican-Americans in the United States was brought about by the country's work-force needs that resulted in large migrations from Mexico during certain time periods. This was particularly true during the building of the railroads in the 1880s and the farm programs of the 1940s. Many of these work programs formalized the entry of large numbers of Mexican nationals to the United States to work in agriculture or industry. Usually workers were poorly paid, experienced minimal job protection, and were quickly deported whenever there were changes in the country's economic picture.

The number of Mexican-Americans has continued to increase. The largely unguarded border between the two countries and the ever-present need for cheap labor (in agriculture, industry, and service fields) make it possible for large numbers of Mexicans to migrate to the United States (in many cases without immigration documents) and to find jobs easily. Continued economic problems in Mexico increased the number of Mexican individuals moving to the United States in recent decades since migration usually meant greater employment and better economic conditions. Due probably to geographic proximity to Mexico, to similarities in weather, and to the existence of large Mexican-American communities, the majority of Mexican-Americans are found in the southwestern United States (California, Texas, New Mexico, Nevada, etc.).

Puerto Ricans

The earliest group of Puerto Ricans in the United States was either part of the revolutionary intelligentsia during the Spanish-American war or was employed as contract sugar workers in Hawaii or cigar makers in Florida, Philadelphia, and New York. Employment opportunities on the mainland served as migratory pulls for Puerto Ricans who moved to New York in significant numbers during the early part of the twentieth century. In 1917, Puerto Ricans were granted U.S. citizenship and were permitted to enter the United States without restrictions. This fact, together with the initiation of low-priced air transportation between Puerto Rico and New York City, marked the beginning of large-scale migration of Puerto Ricans to the continental United States.

During the 1960s and 1970s, many mainland Puerto Ricans migrated back to the island, but this return migration has slowed during the 1980s. In many cases, the availability of low-cost transportation and the presence of familial ties in both places (on the island and the mainland) increased the frequency of return migration from the United States to the island and back to the continental United States.

Cubans

Long-term Cuban migration to the United States is a more recent phenomenon than that of Mexicans and Puerto Ricans, although significant Cuban communities existed in Florida and in New York as early as the 1870s. A large contingent of Cubans initially arrived in the United States in the last few days of the dictatorship of Fulgencio Batista and the first days of the 1959 revolution led by Fidel Castro. These individuals joined some Cubans who had previously migrated to the United States for reasons similar to those influencing other Latin Americans immigrants (family reunification, economic advancement, and educational opportunities). The most recent Cuban immigrants (those arriving since 1980) have been described as having left their country because of the economic hardships imposed on them by the socialist revolution or because of political or philosophical differences with the revolution (Portes & Bach, 1985).

By the end of 1960 and during 1961 and 1962 large numbers of mostly middle-class Cubans arrived in the United States as part of organized resettlement efforts for individuals who disagreed with the revolution led by Fidel Castro. During those years, flights of Cuban refugees arrived on sporadic basis interrupted only by political conflicts between the United States and Cuba. In 1965, refugee flights were re-started and large numbers of Cubans began to arrive once again in the United States, in part due to family reunification efforts. A more recent increase of Cuban immigrants took place in 1980 when approximately 120,000

Cubans arrived in Florida aboard a small flotilla after the Cuban government opened the port of Mariel to those willing to leave the island.

The major waves of Cuban migration have been characterized as involving different types of immigrants (Rogg, 1974). The first were for the most part upper-class Cubans who brought with them their personal fortunes and were familiar with the business world of the United States. The second major group (those leaving after the revolutionary government had been in power for a few months) were largely middle-class professionals and technicians together with skilled and semi-skilled workers. Many of these refugees were unable to take any of their belongings with them but were met with support programs financed by the United States government and certain charitable organizations. The last major group of Cuban refugees, known as "Marielitos" because they left Cuba through the Mariel port, were usually less skilled than the initial refugees, had lived a significant proportion of their lives (approximately 23 years) under a socialist government, and included a large proportion of dark-skinned Cubans.

Many Cuban refugees settled initially in Dade County, Florida, although resettlement efforts were initiated to move them to other states. Currently, the majority of Cubans live in Dade County and in areas of New Jersey and New York although they, like other Hispanic subgroups, can be found in each of the 50 states.

Other Hispanics

"Other Hispanics" is a label of convenience that designates a wide range of individuals who do not trace their family background to Mexico, Cuba, or Puerto Rico. Other Hispanics can be South Americans who have lived in the United States for two generations, or Central Americans who are fleeing the political turmoil of the 1980s and 1990s in their countries.

Understandably then, "Other Hispanics" refers to a very heterogeneous group encompassing professionals, white-collar employees, and blue-collar workers who left their countries in search of better education or employment or in reaction to political changes. Some migrated because of revolutionary or left-leaning governments (for example, Nicaraguans in the 1980s) or to get away from armed political conflicts (for example, Salvadorans in the 1980s), while others came in search of better education for themselves or their children together with better and more stable employment opportunities.

It is important to note that with the exception of Cuba, Mexico, and Puerto Rico, all Latin American countries are represented in this group of "Other Hispanics." According to the 1980 census, the largest groups were from the Dominican Republic, Colombia, Ecuador, El Salvador, Guatemala, Peru, and Nicaragua (Bureau of the Census, 1983).

BASIC HISPANIC CULTURAL VALUES

In addition to having a thorough understanding of the sociodemographic characteristics of Hispanics, researchers must become familiar with certain basic cultural values that may affect the process and outcome of a given study. This section presents a brief summary of some cultural characteristics of Hispanics to consider when formulating a research question, planning data collection methods, and analyzing study results. The presentation of Hispanic cultural values is selective and there is a certain level of disagreement among researchers as to the meaning and implications of some of these values.

Allocentrism

Allocentrism (or collectivism) has been proposed as a basic Hispanic value by a number of researchers, recently by Hofstede (1980). Allocentric societies emphasize the needs, objectives, and points of view of an ingroup while individualistic cultures determine their social behavior primarily in terms of personal objectives, attitudes, and values that resemble little if at all those of the ingroup (Marín & Triandis, 1985). Because it is allocentric, Hispanic culture differs in important ways from the individualistic, competitive, achievement-oriented cultures of the nonminority groups in the United States.

Allocentrism has been associated in previous studies with high levels of personal interdependence, field sensitivity, conformity, readiness to be influenced by others, mutual empathy, willingness to sacrifice for the welfare of the ingroup members, and trust of the members of the ingroup (Marín & Triandis, 1985). Data confirming Hispanics as allocentric have been obtained by Hofstede (1980) among executives of a large transnational corporation in more than 40 different countries as well as by Marín and Triandis (1985) among large numbers of young adults in the United States and in Latin America.

Research has shown that because of allocentrism, Hispanics prefer interpersonal relationships in ingroups that are nurturing, loving, intimate, and respectful while non-Hispanic Whites prefer confrontational and superordinated relationships (Triandis, Marín, Hui, Lisansky, & Ottati, 1984). This pattern for preferred interpersonal relationships can be of significance in designing research projects with Hispanics since it makes explicit the need for friendly interactions between researcher and respondent as well as the effectiveness of research approaches that enhance personal contact. These same values can also be problematic for researchers since allocentrism may move Hispanic respondents to provide the researcher with biased responses (e.g., socially desirable answers) in order to promote the nurturing nature of the encounter. As a matter of fact, Hofstede (1980) has found that allocentric individuals produced higher levels of acquiescent responses when responding to questionnaires than did individuals coming from less collectivistic nations. A recent study (Marín, Gamba & Marín, in press) documents this behavior among Hispanics.

Simpatía

"*Simpatía*" is a Hispanic cultural script that is probably derived from the allocentrism value. *Simpatía* emphasizes the need for behaviors that promote smooth and pleasant social relationships. As a script, *simpatía* moves the individual to show a certain level of conformity and empathy for the feelings of other people. In addition, a person with *simpatía* ("*simpático*") behaves with dignity and respect toward others and strives to achieve harmony in interpersonal relations. Researchers have operationally defined *simpatía* as a general tendency toward avoiding interpersonal conflict, emphasizing positive behaviors in agreeable situations, and de-emphasizing negative behaviors in conflictive circumstances (Triandis, Marín, Lisansky, & Betancourt, 1984).

Various aspects of the *simpatía* script have been documented by researchers. The avoidance of confrontation and other negative aspects of conflictive situations has been shown in a number of studies dealing with conflict resolution (e.g., Kagan, Knight, & Martinez-Romero, 1982; Kagan & Madsen, 1971). Another study has demonstrated the overall preference for avoiding interpersonal conflict in a variety of social situations regardless of the type of actors and the circumstances (Triandis, Marín, Lisansky, & Betancourt, 1984).

Simpatía as well as allocentrism may be responsible for greater socially desirable responses by Hispanic respondents (see Chapter 6) and for differences in how aggressive and assertive behaviors are perceived by Hispanics. A primary implication of this cultural script is the need for researchers to establish positive relationships with Hispanic respondents. As suggested in later chapters, *simpatía* affects subject recruitment and retention, as well as refusal rates and the validity and reliability of the data. In household interviews for example, it would not be uncommon for Hispanics to offer the interviewer coffee or a snack as an expression of *simpatía*. Because of the importance of the social script, respondents will be unhappy if their offering is not accepted. Small talk (known as *"la plática"* in Mexico) before and after an interview will also facilitate respondent satisfaction and cooperation and will build empathetic relationships between researcher and respondent. *Simpatía* also may play a role in the low refusal rates usually found among Hispanics (see Chapter 3) and in the ease of obtaining promises to participate in research that later may not be fulfilled (e.g., participants who fail to return for a follow-up interview).

Familialism

The value of familialism has been proposed as one of the most important culture-specific values of Hispanics (Moore, 1970). A number of authors have also argued that this value is central to specific Hispanic subgroups such as Mexican-Americans (Alvirez & Bean, 1976), Puerto Ricans (Glazer & Moynihan, 1963), Cubans (Szapocznik & Kurtines, 1980), and Central and South Americans (Cohen, 1979). A recent market research study conducted with a national representative sample of Hispanics showed that indeed familialism, together with a desire for a better life and a belief in self-determination, is one of the key Hispanic values ("Advertisers Study," 1989).

Familialism (also called "familism" or *"familismo"*) is a cultural value that involves individuals' strong identification with and attachment to their nuclear and extended families, and strong feelings of loyalty, reciprocity, and solidarity among members of the same family (Triandis, Marín, Betancourt, Lisansky, & Chang, 1982). This value appears to help protect individuals against physical and emotional stress (Cohen, 1979; Grebler, Moore, & Guzman, 1970) by providing natural support systems (Cohen, 1979; Mannino & Shore, 1976; Valle & Martinez, 1980).

Familialism has been shown (Sabogal, Marín, Otero-Sabogal, Marín & Pérez-Stable, 1987) to include three types of value orientations: (a) perceived obligations to provide material and emotional support to the members of the extended family; (b) reliance on relatives for help and support; and (c) the perception of relatives as behavioral and attitudinal referents. These aspects are found among all Hispanic groups and tend to remain personally significant independent of the number of years individuals have lived in the United States or of their generational history.

Familialism also manifests itself in close relationships and involvement with the members of the extended family, which is made up of blood relatives as well as of fictive kin—a special category of kinship that exists among Hispanics and among other allocentric cultures. *"Compadres"* and *"comadres"* are those close family friends who are given the status of relatives (co-parents, literally) due to especially close friendships or to their involvement in the raising of children (e.g., as godparents in a child's baptism). These fictive kin are treated like family members in most respects.

Researchers working with Hispanic populations will find that an understanding of and respect for familialism is helpful. In formulating research questions, investigators should carefully consider how this marked emphasis on the obligations to and support from the family will affect other psychological variables being studied. In our research developing behavior change interventions we have found that the identification of the particular consequences of the behavior change on the family can be crucial in motivating change (Marín, Marín, Pérez-Stable, Otero-Sabogal, & Sabogal, 1990). Family-related reasons for smoking cessation (e.g., bad example to the children, effects of smoking on family's health) were found to be far more important for Hispanic than non-Hispanic White smokers. Appeals to family values or incentives, such as small gifts to the children or relatives, also can motivate respondents to participate in research projects.

Power Distance

Hofstede (1980) has suggested that "power distance" is another important cultural value that differentiates cultural groups. The construct of power distance is defined as a measure of interpersonal power or influence that exists between two individuals. This cultural value supports the notion that societies have powerful individuals as a result of inherent traits (e.g., intelligence) or of inherited or acquired characteristics (e.g., money, education). These individuals strive to maintain their power in relationship to those less powerful, and societies as a rule tend to support these power differentials (e.g., between the well educated and the less informed or between the rich and the poor).

Societies can differ in the degree to which they support the existence of power differentials (i.e., power distance) by promoting deference and respect toward certain powerful groups or individuals (e.g., the rich, the educated, the aged) or even toward certain professions (e.g., physicians, priests, teachers). Hofstede's research has shown that individuals from high power-distance cultures, Hispanics among them, value conformity and obedience and support autocratic and authoritarian attitudes from those in charge of organizations or institutions. There is also a general fear of disagreeing with those in power among individuals from high power distance cultures. The less powerful in such cultures try to meet all of the expectations of the powerful members of society.

In groups with high power distance, the maintenance of personal respect ("*respeto*") in interpersonal relations allows individuals to feel that their personal power, whatever it may be, is being acknowledged. This is particularly important in the treatment of strangers. Investigators must design research procedures that acknowledge and respect the social power of the research participants and permit face-saving in the disclosure of personal information. Another important derivation of this cultural value is the deference that Hispanic respondents may show for a researcher that comes from outside the community, a reaction that needs to be carefully handled so as to avoid feelings of exploitation on the part of the community members.

Personal Space

The anthropological writings of Edward T. Hall (1969) have suggested that different cultures have specific preferences in terms of the amount of physical space they consider appropriate between people when they are interacting. In general, Hispanics have been shown to prefer shorter distances than non-Hispanic Whites. Hispanics, like other "contact cultures," feel comfortable when physically close to others and are less likely to feel that their personal space has been invaded when a stranger comes close to them.

Differences in personal space are important to understand because they affect the emotional reactions of individuals to a given social interaction. Non-Hispanics who prefer to stand farther apart than Hispanics may find themselves inexplicably uncomfortable with Hispanics who seem pushy by their insistence on establishing closer interpersonal spacing. At the same time, Hispanics may often find non-Hispanics to be cold and distant because of their need for more physical distance. The implications of these feelings for establishing rapport in an interview can easily be seen.

Time Orientation

The observation that cultures differ in terms of temporal orientation has been present in the literature of the social sciences for some time (e.g., Kluckhohn & Strodtbeck, 1961). Certain cultures in the United States are considered future-oriented due to their emphasis on planning for the future and being able to delay gratification as well as on punctuality and efficiency. In contrast, present-oriented societies are often described as unable to delay gratification or to plan for the future and as inefficient and not punctual. A number of researchers (Hall, 1983) have suggested that Hispanics and Latin Americans can be considered present-oriented and that this cultural value translates into often being late for appointments (Levine, West, & Reis, 1980) or in misperceiving the length of time spent at a task (Holtzman, Diaz-Guerrero, & Swartz, 1975).

Hispanics tend to have a more flexible attitude toward time than non-Hispanic Whites, particularly concerning events or activities that do not necessarily demand punctuality (e.g., attending a party or a social function, meeting a friend). This flexibility allows Hispanics to feel they are on time even if they arrive 15 or 20 minutes after the appointed time (Marín, 1987). Of particular significance in terms of time orientation is the fact that Hispanics place greater value on the quality of interpersonal relationships than on the length of time in which they take place. This cultural trait has significant implications for research projects in which appointments are made for interviews or observations. Highly efficient or time conscious researchers may be perceived as impolite or insulting by Hispanic respondents. Likewise, researchers should not feel that the participants have decided not to participate in the investigation if they fail to appear at the exact time of the appointment.

Gender Roles

Like all cultures, Hispanics have defined gender-related behaviors for both men and women. Much has been written about Hispanic men and the assumed cultural expectations for being strong, in control, and the providers for their families ("machismo"). Traditionally, Hispanic women are described as submissive and lacking in power and influence (Heller, 1966; Madsen, 1961). Nevertheless, these stereotypic perceptions of male-female relationships among Hispanics have not been fully documented (Amaro, 1988; Heller, 1966). Cromwell and Ruiz (1979), for example, have shown that across studies, male dominance in marital decision making is absent among Hispanic couples.

While the actual validity or prevalence of the stereotypic machismo is unknown, a male Hispanic may view an interviewer of either gender who wishes to speak to his wife with suspicion and may actually forbid her from participating in a study. These gender roles may affect subject sampling and selection if the male in a household prevents other family members from participating in a study if he feels that his role is to interpret the feelings of the other family members. In our experience in studying Hispanics we have found this attitude to be present but not very prevalent. In rare cases, husbands have not allowed us to talk to their wives as part of an interview or wives have indicated that they feel uncomfortable talking to an interviewer until after their husbands have given their approval.

This first chapter has presented a brief overview of the demographic and cultural characteristics of Hispanics in the United States. The similarities based on shared cultural traditions and history are the basis for considering well over 20 million residents of the United States as part of a single ethnic group. At the same time, this is not a monolithic group; there are important differences across individuals and among specific subgroups based on such characteristics as national origin, migration and generational history, religious faith, and linguistic preferences. Researchers working with Hispanics will need to understand not only the sociodemographic characteristics of Hispanics but also their cultural values and norms. The information included here can serve as an outline to the areas that need to be covered in properly understanding and conducting research with Hispanics.

2

Issues in Identifying Hispanics

An important aspect of any research project is the definition of the parameters to be utilized in selecting the sample of respondents, consultants, or subjects who will take part in the study. Among those variables that are usually considered important in the social and behavioral sciences are respondent characteristics such as age, gender, marital status, level of education, occupation, and socioeconomic status.

When a research project deals with racial or ethnic groups, investigators need to consider additional characteristics that help to identify the individuals who are going to be studied. While in some cases race or linguistic considerations may be sufficient to identify prospective participants, such clearly defined characteristics are not appropriate for studies with Hispanics. This chapter describes the various ways in which previous researchers have operationalized Hispanic ethnicity. In addition, and given that not all Hispanics are alike (Chapter 1), within-group heterogeneity (i.e., in terms of acculturation level, national origin, generation or migrational history) will be discussed as it may be a relevant variable when designing sampling strategies and analyzing data. Finally, those circumstances in which a researcher can talk about Hispanics as a group will be identified together with situations in which it is essential to differentiate among the various Hispanic subgroups (e.g., Mexican-Americans as different from Puerto Ricans, Cubans, or Central or South Americans).

CHOOSING THE APPROPRIATE LABEL

Probably the first concern of a researcher trying to study Hispanics is deciding on the ethnic label to be utilized in describing the participants or searching for data in archival research. We have chosen to use the label "Hispanic" in this book to refer to those residents of the United States who trace their family background to one of the Spanish-speaking Latin American nations or to Spain. Nevertheless, this label is not only very recent but it is not universally accepted by the individuals it is used to describe. As a matter of fact, a number of other labels have been used in the literature to refer to this ethnic group (e.g., Latino, Raza, Spanish-speaking, Spanish-surnamed, Latin, Spanish, Latin American, Chicano) and arguments have frequently been presented for the advantages of one over another of these labels (e.g., Hayes-Bautista & Chapa, 1987; Treviño, 1987).

The discussion that follows presents a short overview of the uses and limitations of the various labels that refer to Hispanics in the United States. Survey researchers, anthropologists, and other social, behavioral, and health scientists interested in interviewing Hispanic respondents will need to understand the meaning of the ethnic labels that respondents assign to themselves as these usually correspond to important aspects of their self-concept. Investigators using archival data (Stewart, 1984) will need to be familiar with the usage of the various labels in order to understand properly the characteristics of the individuals studied and to establish the comparability of various data sets. Although Shakespeare felt that "a rose by any other name would smell as sweet," it seems that labels that human groups assign to themselves are much more meaningful than the names we give other objects. As a matter of fact, psychological research has clearly shown that different group labels produce differential attitudinal responses among those who use them (e.g., Brewer & Brewer, 1971; Marín, 1984). The following paragraphs attest to this phenomenon among Hispanics.

Central to any discussion of ethnic group labels is the identification of those characteristics that should be considered to define group membership. As Hayes-Bautista and Chapa (1987) have argued, these characteristics can be shared language, surnames, type of ancestors, national origin, or religious traditions and practices. For Hispanics, the central element to define group membership seems to be the national origin of the individuals or of their families or ancestors.

National origin or ancestry seems to be a better criterion to establish group membership when identifying Hispanics because other criteria are not inclusive enough: Not all Hispanics speak Spanish; Spanish surnames are often shared by the Portuguese, French, Pilipinos, and Italians; not all Hispanics descend from one identical ancestral tradition, be it European or Native American; and not all Hispanics are Roman Catholics or were raised as Roman Catholics. Given these possible criteria for defining ethnicity, it seems safe to argue that national origin (either personal or ancestral) is the element that best defines Hispanics in the United States.

Nevertheless, this criterion of ancestry is sometimes not sufficiently clear or specific since individuals born in a Latin American country may not necessarily share the cultural roots of the majority of Latin Americans. This becomes evident when one considers the children born to European immigrants in one of the Latin American countries that received heavy European migrations during World War II (e.g., Cuba, Argentina, Paraguay, Uruguay, Chile). Though these individuals may have been born in Latin America, their parents or grandparents were born and raised in a European country different from Spain and may have heavily influenced family customs, traditions, and values to create a context for that child that is very different from that experienced by other Latin Americans. The number of Hispanics who have experienced these conditions is comparatively small; still, it is a problem that needs to be taken into consideration when doing research with Hispanics in the United States.

The confusion of ethnicity with race or national origin was prominent in official government studies and data reports until the 1940 census when "Mexican" stopped being listed as a race and Hispanics were enumerated as White. Nevertheless, it was not until the 1970 census that the federal government tried to study Hispanics separately from other ethnic groups. The 1970 census used several different definitions for the "Spanish heritage population." In the southwestern states, those individuals who were Spanish-surnamed or who spoke Spanish were considered Hispanics. Puerto Rican birth or parentage was the criterion in the three mid-Atlantic states while only Spanish language fluency was used in the remaining states (Bureau of the Census, 1979).

Hispanic

"Hispanic" as an ethnic label is the product of a decision by the Office of Management and Budget (OMB) in 1978 to operationalize the label as "A person of Mexican, Puerto Rican, Cuban, Central or South American or other Spanish culture or origin, regardless of race" (*Federal Register,* 1978, p. 19269). The word is supposed to be a derivation of the Latin word for Spain (*Hispania*) that at times has also been used to describe the whole Iberian peninsula (Spain, Portugal, and Andorra). The Royal Academy of the Spanish Language further defines those individuals born in the Spanish-speaking countries south of the Rio Grande as "*Hispanoamericanos*" lending support to the appropriateness of the use of "Hispanic" to refer to individuals who trace their ancestral background to one of those countries in the Americas.

As can be expected with any label of convenience, the emergence of the label "Hispanic" has created confusion in the application of the OMB criteria as well as cogent arguments for its rejection (Hayes-Bautista & Chapa, 1987; Pérez-Stable, 1987). Among the difficulties in applying the OMB criteria, the most serious problem emerges in classifying those individuals whose family origin is directly associated with Spain and not with Latin America. As part of the OMB definition, those individuals could be considered Hispanic since they would be covered by the provision of "other Spanish culture or origin." Nevertheless, some authors have argued that those individuals who trace their family background to Spain have historical, cultural, and demographic characteristics that make them very different from those Hispanics whose ancestry is in Latin America. This issue is important since a significant proportion of U.S. Hispanics of Cuban and Argentinian background have had parents who were born in Spain. In addition, a number of immigrants from Spain reside in the United States and could very well self-identify as Hispanics.

An additional difficulty with the OMB definition of "Hispanic" is deciding if those individuals who trace their family background to Belize, Brazil, the Guyanas, Portugal, Cape Verde, or the Philippines should be considered Hispanics. In the case of Brazil and Portugal it could be argued that while Spanish culture or origin are absent, the two Iberian countries have shared not only substantial cultural traditions but historically have shared governments, commerce, and derivations of the language. Pilipinos could consider themselves Hispanic since many have indeed shared in the Spanish culture during the years of Spanish occupation of their islands, a fact that influenced their language, traditions, and culture. While these arguments have some relative validity, the spirit if not the letter of the OMB regulation excludes Brazilians, Portuguese, Cape Verdeans, and Pilipinos from the "Hispanic" label.

Latino

The label "Latino" has been proposed recently by a number of individuals including various social scientists (Hayes-Bautista & Chapa, 1987; Pérez-Stable, 1987). This label is perceived as more accurately reflecting the political, geographical, and historical links present among the various Latin American nations. Hayes-Bautista and Chapa also argue that "Latino" is the best label to describe Hispanics since it preserves national origin of the referents as a significant characteristic, it is culturally and racially neutral, and may be the least objectionable of all possible ethnic labels.

While the Latino label is certainly appealing to many, problems are encountered when it is operationalized. Hayes-Bautista and Chapa (1987) suggested that Latinos are those born in any of the Latin American nations regardless of the language spoken there. This definition includes as Latinos those individuals born in Portuguese- and English-speaking countries such as Brazil, Belize, and the Guyanas but excludes Spaniards, Portuguese, and Pilipinos. In addition, its use produces some important discrepancies with the official criteria developed by the U.S. OMB for the label "Hispanic."

Treviño (1987) has argued that the label "Latino" is inappropriate for pragmatic reasons. Most of the data on Hispanics are collected by the U.S. government and other agencies following the OMB definition and therefore they use "Hispanic" rather than "Latino." Divergent terminology and definitional criteria can only add confusion, as Treviño suggests. A further problem also mentioned by Treviño with the adoption of "Latino" as a label for Hispanics is the fact that those who self-identify as "Latino" may not necessarily be the same as individuals who self-identify as "Hispanic." These differences in self-identification could render the labels not interchangeable and the samples too unique to be comparable.

In addition, Treviño (1987) suggests that a careful reading of the etymology of "Latino" would force us to accept as Hispanics those individuals who trace their cultural roots to European Roman/Latin influence (France, Italy, Rumania, Spain, Portugal). This extension would, of course, eliminate the purpose of the label as perceived by Hayes-Bautista and Chapa (1987)-that is, specifically trying to limit it to cover only those who trace their ancestry to the Americas.

A recent editorial in a scientific journal dealing with the problems of ethnic labels (Yankauer, 1987) suggested that insights could be gained by asking respondents how they wished to be labeled. An unpublished *Los Angeles Times* poll found that similar proportions of Hispanic respondents favored the labels "Latino" and "Hispanic." Non-Hispanic Whites in the same poll preferred to use "Hispanic" over "Latino." Recently we conducted a survey among a representative sample of 700 Hispanics in San Francisco and found that the less acculturated Hispanics tended to prefer the label "Latino" in somewhat greater proportions (57%) than the more acculturated respondents (43%). The label "Hispanic" was preferred by 41% of the less acculturated and 53% of the more acculturated respondents. Interestingly, very few respondents (3%) felt that it did not matter which label was used to describe Hispanics in the United States.

Chicano and Raza

As mentioned above, other labels have been used to refer to Hispanics as a whole. Two labels should be mentioned here since they have been frequently used in the scientific literature although their use is less common at present: "Chicano" and "Raza." In many cases these labels reflect a certain political and social consciousness on the part of the researchers at a time when a unifying label such as "Hispanic" was not available. The label "Chicano" has often been used inappropriately in the literature to refer to Hispanics as a whole, ignoring the fact that it only refers to individuals who trace their family background to Mexico. In addition, the label "Chicano" is heavily loaded with negative stereotypes and surplus meaning when used by non-Hispanics (Fairchild & Cozens, 1981; Marín, 1984), a fact that limits its usefulness in social science research. For example, in a study with non-Hispanic college students in California, a significant proportion of the respondents (64%) felt that an important characteristic of "Chicanos" was to be aggressive while only 26% of the same respondents assigned aggressiveness to the label "Mexican-Americans" (Marín, 1984). In the overall evaluation of both labels using a semantic differential, "Mexican-American" obtained significantly more positive evaluation than did "Chicano" when rated by the same individuals.

The label "Raza" as a way to denote Hispanics in social science and public health research has been proposed by Hayes-Bautista (1980) and has been used by some researchers and particularly by individuals in the southwestern states. This is probably the least common of all the alternative labels discussed here for denoting those individuals who trace their ancestral roots to Latin America.

Given the need to identify respondents properly, and until a better label is developed (as is currently happening in the United States, where African-American is replacing Black), investigators may keep in mind the OMB definition:

"Hispanic" refers to "a person of Mexican, Puerto Rican, Cuban, Central or South American or other Spanish culture or origin, regardless of race."

In choosing a label to denote those individuals who reside in the United States and who trace their family background to Latin America or Spain, researchers should keep the following in mind:

"Hispanic" (or "Latino") is a label used to refer to an ethnic category and not to a race.

If a study deals with only one Hispanic subgroup (e.g., Mexican-Americans, Puerto Ricans) the sample should be described by that subgroup label and not by the generic "Hispanic" or "Latino" label. This prevents unwarranted overgeneralizations.

If researchers are interested in obtaining an indication of the racial characteristics of Hispanics, probably the best way to gather that information is by using the questions utilized in the decennial census ("Is this person White, Black, American Indian, Asian or Pacific Islander, Other?"). Nevertheless, investigators should remember that this particular question (at least as used in the 1980 and 1990 census) seems to be inappropriate to some Hispanics. Approximately 40% of Hispanic respondents wrote their national or familial origin in the race question rather than choosing a racial label such as White or Black (Tienda & Ortiz, 1986).

OPERATIONALIZATION OF HISPANIC ETHNICITY

Once a decision has been made as to the label to be used in identifying Hispanics as an ethnic group, investigators need to consider the ways in which that label is to be operationalized. This is an important decision since it affects the quality of the data as well as the generalizability of the results of the study. Furthermore, a clear specification of the criteria used is essential in allowing future readers and investigators to compare their results with those of previous studies (Hayes-Bautista, 1983). In general, there are three ways in which Hispanic ethnicity can be operationalized: ancestry, cultural characteristics, and self-identification. Each of these is discussed below in detail.

Ancestry

Although the operationalization of ancestry or national origin can at times be difficult, considering all alternatives, ancestry is probably the best characteristic to identify Hispanics in a sample of respondents. As a matter of fact, the 1980 and 1990 censuses used only ancestry in identifying Hispanics from among the smaller sample of respondents who answered the long form of the census questionnaire. The short form (answered by all residents of the country) utilized self-identification as the primary question followed by some general ancestry questions. An advantage of using ancestry as an identifier is the fact that this is an area in a person's background where investigators can usually expect true and honest responses.

In general, Hispanic ancestry can be identified by asking respondents to report their place of birth and that of their parents and grandparents. But the use of these responses requires the researcher to establish specific parameters for considering a respondent as Hispanic. When the respondents or their parents are born in Latin America or in Spain, they would be unequivocally considered as Hispanics. But when the actual migration to the United States took place three or more generations before the respondent's birth, misclassifications can arise. The limitation to three generations, while done to avoid burdening respondents with a long list of similar questions, is not only arbitrary but may also fail to reflect the actual ethnic loyalty that a person may feel toward the family's ancestral home. For example, individuals whose great-grandparents migrated from Mexico may consider themselves Hispanic even if all relatives since then have been born in the United States. Unfortunately, the criterion mentioned above (three-generation ancestry) would classify this person as non-Hispanic. What this example shows is the need for specific criteria to be used in describing a sample and in comparing the results from different studies since misclassifications can easily occur.

In some cases it may become useful or necessary to identify the specific Hispanic subgroup ancestry of the individuals who participated in a study in order to differentiate, for example, Mexican-Americans from Puerto Ricans. The 1980 census question that asks a respondent to indicate if he or she is of Hispanic origin and then to indicate the specific subgroup ("Mexican, Mexican-American, Chicano"; "Puerto Rican"; "Cuban"; or "Other Spanish/Hispanic") may help researchers to obtain that information. An alternative is the question used in the Hispanic Health and Nutrition Examination Survey (H-HANES; National Center for Health Statistics, 1985). This national study focused on only three Hispanic subgroups (Cuban-Americans, Mexican-Americans, and Puerto Ricans) and used ancestry of self, mother, and father as well as place of birth of mother and father as a way to establish subgroup ancestry. For each individual, respondents were asked to indicate their "ethnic identity" by choosing one of 13 different labels ("Boricuan," "Puerto Rican," "Cuban," "Cuban-American," "Mexican/Mexicano," "Chicano," "Mexican-American," "Hispano," "Latin American," "Other Spanish or Hispanic," "American," "Anglo-American," "Other group"). Unfortunately, such questions have the problem of utilizing specific subgroup labels (some of them neologisms in English—"Boricuan," and in Spanish—"Hispano") that may inappropriately describe the respondent's background or that may carry surplus meaning. In addition, it requires that the respondent understand the meaning of a complex social science construct such as "ethnic identity."

An approach to identifying Hispanic subgroup ancestry for those Hispanics who were born in the United States is presented in Figure 2.1. This question has been utilized with success in both communitywide surveys conducted over the telephone (Marín, Pérez-Stable, & Marín, 1989) and face-to-face studies. It asks respondents to identify their country of ancestry. When individuals have mixed Hispanic subgroup ancestry (due to intermarriage in the United States or abroad), respondents are asked to identify the ancestry of most of their relatives or the ancestry with which they identify more closely. While this is a simple question that is easy for Hispanics to answer under situations of limited communication, it has the disadvantage that misclassification can also occur, primarily among those of mixed ancestry (e.g., when a Mexican has married a Puerto Rican).

Sociocultural Characteristics

Another way in which the label "Hispanic" can be operationalized is by using such sociocultural characteristics as language use and Spanish language surname. In these cases, respondents are asked to report their experiences with Spanish (e.g., Did they speak it as a child? How fluent are they at the time of the study?) or are asked to provide their full name (first name as well as paternal and maternal surnames). While these options are attractive because of their simplicity, they have important limitations that are discussed below.

Spanish-language surname. A large number of researchers have utilized Spanish-language surname as a way of identifying Hispanics. This approach utilizes lists of surnames frequently found among Hispanics or Latin Americans in order to decide if a given respondent should be considered a Hispanic. If the respondent's surname appears in the list,

The families of the majority of people in the United States come from other countries. Where does your family come from?

Las familias de la mayoría de las personas que viven en Los Estados Unidos provienen de otros paises. ¿De dónde viene su familia?

(DO NOT READ ALTERNATIVES.)

(IF MORE THAN ONE IS MENTIONED, ASK FOR COUNTRY THAT MOST OF THE PEOPLE OF HIS/HER FAMILY COME FROM OR THAT THE RESPONDENT FEELS CLOSER TO.

- México
- Cuba
- Puerto Rico
- Central America (Guatemala, El Salvador, Nicaragua, Honduras, Panamá, Costa Rica)
- Spain
- Dominican Republic
- Other (Specify: _____)

Figure 2.1. Hispanic Subgroup Identifier

the individual is considered Hispanic. Unfortunately, most surname lists, including those developed by the Bureau of the Census are not comprehensive enough since they exclude a significant proportion of surnames and those included in the list lend themselves to a number of misclassification errors.

The limitations inherent in the use of surnames to choose a sample can best be seen in a study by the Bureau of the Census that showed that about one-third of those who claim Hispanic origin do not have a Spanish-language surname. Furthermore, one-third of those who have Spanish-language surnames do not consider themselves Hispanic (Bureau of the Census, 1973). Other studies have shown that the misclassification rates when surnames are used can be lower than those found in the census studies, particularly when combined with an additional criterion such as language spoken as a child (Aday, Chiu, & Andersen, 1980; Shlifer & Barrios, 1974).

One of the most significant possibilities for error in using surname lists is misclassification due to migration and intermarriage of a respondent's ancestors. It is possible, for example, for Hispanics to have non-Spanish-language surnames (particularly among individuals with Argentinian, Chilean, Uruguayan, Venezuelan, and Paraguayan ancestry) that would exclude them from a sample based on such criterion. Non-Spanish surnames (e.g., Banchs, Dols, Galtieri, Cristiani, Domecq) are frequently found among Latin Americans but are not found in the Spanish surname lists often used to select samples. Many of these cases can be found among Hispanics who trace their ancestry to countries with significant migrations from Italy, Germany, the United Kingdom, and other non-Iberian countries.

A second problem with the use of surname lists is the fact that non-Hispanic women may acquire a Spanish-language surname through marriage and non-Hispanic children through adoption. These facts would artificially augment the number of Hispanics in a sample and could seriously bias the responses obtained in a study. There is indeed some evidence that Hispanics out-marry with frequency, particularly among second- and higher-generation Hispanics (Mittlebach & Moore, 1968). This substantial number of non-Hispanics with Spanish surnames could present a serious problem in terms of data validity. In addition, Hispanic women who marry non-Hispanics usually lose their surname and would not be identified as Hispanics through this approach.

Additional errors in the use of surname lists are produced by those Hispanics who have anglicized their surname or changed it to an English-language surname for professional use (e.g., Charlie Sheen) or for other personal reasons. Finally, certain individuals born to Hispanic mothers and to non-Hispanic fathers will not carry a Spanish-language surname although they may feel, behave, and self-identify as Hispanics.

A study comparing the census list of Spanish surnames (Bureau of the Census, 1980) with a computerized program (Generally Useful Ethnic Search System; GUESS) showed that both approaches performed approximately equally well. The census list, for example, correctly categorized 85% of the males and 79% of the females as Hispanic while the GUESS scores were 87% and 82%, respectively. When both approaches were combined, the accuracy of identification increased to 90% for males and 84% for females (Howard, Samet, Buechley, Schrag, & Key, 1983).

Spanish language use. The gathering of information on language use or proficiency in order to establish Hispanic ethnicity is problematic since Hispanics vary widely in their linguistic proficiency in Spanish as well as in English. While first-generation Hispanics (actual immigrants) may report speaking Spanish as a child and being proficient in

Spanish, this may not be true for second- and third-generation Hispanics whose parents or grandparents may have spoken Spanish but who are not proficient in Spanish themselves. While national data on language proficiency among Hispanics are not available, the 1980 census showed that well over 3 million people (5 years of age and older) speak only English although others in their household speak Spanish (*Hispanic Almanac*, 1984). If those households are assumed to be Hispanic, it could be estimated that at least 20% of Hispanics speak only English.

Non-Hispanics who speak Spanish fluently represent an additional source of misclassification when Spanish language use is the criterion for identification. Using language fluency as the basis for classification, these individuals would be misclassified as Hispanics, thus artificially inflating the number of Hispanic respondents and seriously biasing the results of a study. While their numbers may not be very large, non-Hispanics fluent in Spanish could provide enough bias in a sample to make the results of a study suspect. This phenomenon may be particularly serious in those areas of the country where the proportion of Hispanics is significant and where Spanish has become a prominent language for business transactions (e.g., parts of California, Florida, New York, New Jersey, and Texas).

Self-Identification

An additional approach to operationalizing Hispanic ethnicity is to ask those individuals who are planning to participate in a study if they consider themselves to be Hispanic or Latino. This approach has the obvious limitation that some individuals may identify with a specific subgroup label (e.g., Mexican-Americans, Cubans, Dominicans) and not use the larger, more encompassing labels. An additional limitation to this approach is the fact that some respondents may dislike these labels and would reply negatively to that type of query. In spite of these limitations, self-identification seems to be a useful if somewhat unreliable approach to identifying Hispanics for research in the social and behavioral sciences.

Analyses of the 1980 census data showed that 6% of those who self-identified as Hispanics did not report any specific Hispanic identifiers (place of birth, ancestry, language, or surname) and thus were probably non-Hispanics (Tienda & Ortiz, 1986). Among those who did not self-identify as Hispanics but who could be considered Hispanic given their responses to other parts of the census form, 11% reported two or more Hispanic identifiers with almost three fourths reporting

Hispanic nationality and/or ancestry. These latter individuals could, therefore, be assumed to be Hispanics who were missed by the main self-identification question. Approximately half of those who did not consider themselves to be Hispanic but who reported a Hispanic identifier reported use of Spanish language and another 19% reported a Spanish surname—characteristics that can be acquired (by schooling or by marriage) without implying actual Hispanic ethnicity.

A further concern with self-identification is the fact that labels used by scientists may have different meanings when used by "people on the street." While the meaning of "Hispanic" may be clear to social scientists, individuals outside of academia may be responding to a different reality when asked if they consider themselves to be Hispanic. In addition, misclassifications can be produced by the fact that people's self-identity may change over time as a function of personal growth, prejudice, changes in life-style, and so on. The 1980 census, for example, showed that foreign-born Hispanics were more consistent in considering themselves Hispanics than were those born in the United States (Giachello, Bell, Aday, & Andersen, 1983).

The problems with labels that identify Hispanics as a whole are also present for the labels chosen for specific Hispanic subgroups. Our analysis of the H-HANES data for the Southwest showed that the respondents' generation was closely associated with their preferred label. Overall, 87% of first-generation respondents preferred to use the label "Mexican" to define themselves while 81% of the second-generation respondents chose "Mexican-American." In addition, a minimal proportion of first- (<1%) and second- (3%) generation respondents chose "Chicano" as a self-identification label.

As seen from the above discussion, the operationalization of "Hispanic" is a difficult task due to the limitations of the criteria that can be used and the fact that investigators need to rely on the respondents' self-report. Nevertheless, researchers may wish to keep these guidelines in mind:

> When time constraints are present, Hispanic ethnicity may be established by asking respondents if they self-identify as "Hispanic" or "Latino."
>
> A more comprehensive and reliable operationalization of the label "Hispanic" can be obtained by producing indices that take into consideration various criteria such as (a) birthplace of self and parents, (b) self-identification, and (c) ancestry.

Use of Spanish surname lists should be avoided. When necessary (e.g., archival research where no other Hispanic identifier is present), at least two surname lists should be consulted.

Researchers may present respondents with the OMB definition of Hispanic and ask respondents if they fit the parameters. In this fashion, personal reactions by the respondents to the label "Hispanic" may be obviated.

HISPANIC HETEROGENEITY

As implied in the OMB definition of "Hispanic," the label refers to a fairly large group of individuals (over 22 million) who share certain specific characteristics. This common background is based on at least 500 years of shared cultural influences predicated on a common language, the historical influence of a colonizing nation (Spain), and the shaping of values and world views by Roman Catholicism. The mixture of these Iberian influences together with the important native cultures and the imported African influences that came with slavery produced a group of nations that share more cultural traits than are found among other countries that share national borders in Europe, Asia, or Africa. The end product is a supranational identity (as Latin Americans) that acknowledges the presence of common cultural threads among those individuals born in one of the 20 nations that make up Spanish-speaking Latin America. These common cultural characteristics go beyond shared language, religious beliefs, types of political institutions, and ideals; they include certain values and beliefs that are central to a human being. Among these values are precepts related to the way people react toward others such as the values of *respeto* and *dignidad* and the social script of *simpatía*. Also shared by Hispanics are the role and personal value of the family, or familialism; the significance of ingroup referents (allocentrism); and the other cultural values mentioned in Chapter 1.

While those common cultural experiences may have produced a Latin American weltanschauung, history interacting with specific environments can be expected to have introduced modifications to those early nations and to their cultures so that differences among them can be easily identified at the present time. These modifications to the Latin American world view allow us to identify particular national characters for the various Latin American countries as well as nation-specific attitudes. Indeed, various authors have studied the characteristics of some nationalities as different from other Latin American groups. Detailed analyses are available for Brazilians (Leite, 1976), Mexicans (Bejar Navarro, 1986; Diaz-Guerrero, 1982; Fromm & Maccoby, 1973; Ramírez, 1977), Chileans (Godoy, 1976), and Colombians (López de Mesa, 1975), among others.

Once individuals migrate to the United States, the new culture and the experiences of adjusting to new environments can be expected to change people's behavior as well as their world views. Of concern for those wishing to study Hispanics in the United States is the degree to which the culture of the United States has influenced Hispanics and to what extent they can be considered a group that shares some central cultural characteristics. The label "Hispanic," as any other name utilized by social and behavioral scientists, is used here and in the literature to refer to individuals who share some characteristics (ethnic, racial, gender, educational, economic, etc.). In this sense, it is a shortcut that allows us to generalize to a population our observations from a sample. Use of the label "Hispanic" should be similar to our use of "male," "Black," "Irish-American," "undergraduate," "gay," or "blue-collar." The label glosses over individual differences in order to allow us to talk in generalities. We want to emphasize that, as with any label of convenience, "Hispanic" reflects the modal characteristics of individuals who of necessity differ among themselves.

There is no doubt that by utilizing large group indicators the characteristics of the smaller units are erased (Castro & Baezconde-Garbanati, 1987). Nevertheless, what needs to be defined is the extent to which the large group can be used as a referent before its usefulness is lost. This concern should be answered based on the actual purpose of the investigation. In some cases it is useful and probably more relevant to talk about the larger group (Hispanic) while in other circumstances the data may yield more significant information when broken down by subgroup (e.g., Mexican-Americans, Cubans). For example, the 1988 Current Population Survey (Bureau of the Census, 1988) showed that the median age of Hispanics (as a whole) was 25.5 years while that of non-Hispanics was 32.9 years. These results show that Hispanics in general are younger than non-Hispanics. At the same time, the same census report showed that the median age for Cuban-Americans was 38.7 years while the median age for Mexican-Americans was 23.9 years. These results show that different perspectives can be gained on the same problem depending on how groups are defined.

The above example on median age of Hispanics can also be used to illustrate the problems that can occur when investigators neglect to explore subgroup characteristics. If the only results reported by the Bureau of the Census had been the median age for Hispanics as a whole, we would have been left with the false impression that most Hispanics are younger than non-Hispanics, while it is clear that one subgroup (Cubans) is older than the nation's non-Hispanics. The importance of these decisions on group definition can be seen when such data are used in governmental decisions for targeting services such as supplemental pay, food allowances, health benefits, and transportation services for the aged.

To make matters more difficult for researchers working with Hispanics, arguments can also be made that important differences are found among subgroups not only in terms of ancestry (for example Mexican-Americans as different from Puerto Ricans) but also in terms of other significant characteristics that define the group to be studied or described. These variables can include race, self-identification (e.g., Mexican-American or Chicano), immigration status, generation, and acculturation level (Castro & Baezconde-Garbanati, 1987; Hayes-Bautista, 1983). The question is how thinly should researchers cut the pie before they are left with only crumbs.

It is beyond the scope of this book to identify all the differences and similarities that exist among Hispanic, but three areas deserve special mention since they have been found to affect significantly the results of various studies with Hispanics: ancestry, generational history, and acculturation level.

Ancestry

Chapter 1 presented an overview of the main national or ancestral groups that can be considered when studying Hispanics. As mentioned there, these groups are usually formed in terms of national (e.g., Cubans, Mexican-Americans) or regional (e.g., Central Americans) origin. Interestingly, the various ancestry groups have been shown to have different demographic and socioeconomic characteristics as well as to exhibit different behaviors.

The Bureau of the Census reports show that the various Hispanic subgroups differ among themselves. Differences in median age have already been mentioned in this chapter. Other interesting differences (Bureau of the Census, 1988) include the fact that the lowest proportion of males is found among Puerto Ricans (46.7%) while the highest (51.5%) is found among Mexican-Americans. Married adults constitute 58.5% of Cubans but only 52.5% of Puerto Ricans. Mexican-Americans have the lowest median number of school years completed (10.8 yrs.) while Central and South Americans and Cubans have the highest (12.4 yrs.). Puerto Ricans have a disproportionately high number of households headed by a woman (44.0%) while Cubans have the lowest (16.1%). Mexican-Americans have the largest mean number of persons per family (4.1) and Cubans have the lowest (3.2).

Differences by Hispanic ancestry also have been found in other areas of research. One significant set of findings addresses the health status of three of the subgroups (Cubans, Mexican-Americans, and Puerto Ricans) primarily as a result of the H-HANES, a cross-sectional study of the health and nutritional status of a large sample of Hispanics. Although the data have not been fully analyzed, a number of important group differences have been reported. For example, 24.5% of Mexican-American women reported smoking cigarettes while approximately 32.6% of Puerto Rican females reported the same behavior at the time of the survey (Escobedo & Remington, 1989). Other large-scale studies have shown that Mexican-American men report heavy drinking of alcoholic beverages in greater proportions (18%) than Puerto Rican (16%) and Cuban-American men (5%) (Caetano, 1986/1987). Another example of subgroup differences is the number of physician visits per year. Mexican-Americans average 3.7 visits while Puerto Ricans average 6.0 and Cuban-Americans 6.2 visits per year. Taken as a whole, Hispanics averaged the same number of visits per year (4.4) as non-Hispanic Whites (4.8) (Treviño, 1984).

Nevertheless, ancestry is not a variable that differentiates all aspects of Hispanic life. Various studies have shown that there are no differences across various Hispanic ancestral groups in the values and attitudes that these individuals hold. For example, in a study on familialism (Sabogal et al., 1987) we have found that Cubans, Central Americans, and Mexican-Americans do not differ in their perceptions and understanding of that cultural value or in the importance of familialism in their personal lives. More relevant in producing statistically significant differences across groups was the acculturation level of the respondents, as the more highly acculturated tended to place less importance on this Hispanic cultural value than did the less acculturated respondents.

Given the above facts, we make this recommendation:

When studying Hispanics, researchers need to establish the ancestry of the respondents studied. This characteristic should be established by requesting information on the birthplace of the respondents as well as on the country of origin of other members of their family.

Generational History

Although less often utilized in research projects, the generational history of the respondents may prove useful for the proper understanding of the characteristics of Hispanic respondents. Establishing the type of generation of a Hispanic respondent or of a group of individuals may clarify some relationships in the data being collected. It is possible, for example, that first-generation Hispanics may behave differently from second-generation Hispanics. As an example, one can consider the differences found in our analysis of the H-HANES data on preferred labels among Mexican-Americans that were reported above. In that data set, the majority of first-generation respondents (87%) preferred to be called "Mexicans" while the majority (81%) of the second-generation participants preferred to be called "Mexican-Americans."

Establishing the generational history of Hispanic respondents is usually easy because it involves asking respondents for their birthplace and that of their parents and grandparents. A faster approach involves asking for the birthplace of the respondents and of their parents and assuming that there is no need to classify properly an individual's generational history beyond the second generation.

Hispanic generational history should be established by asking research participants to identify at a minimum their own birthplace (country) and that of their parents.

When classifying the generational history of respondents, the following labels can be utilized:

First-generation Hispanics: Respondents born in Latin America.

Second-generation Hispanics: Respondents born in the United States and both parents born in Latin America.

Mixed second-generation Hispanics: Respondents born in the United States with one parent born in Latin America.

Third-generation Hispanics: Respondents and both parents born in the United States with all grandparents born in Latin America.

Acculturation Level

As individuals are exposed to a new culture, a process of culture learning and behavioral adaptation takes place (Berry, 1980; Padilla, 1980). This process is usually labeled "acculturation" although the interpretation of the process and the identification and prediction of its outcomes are not universally agreed upon by researchers. In one of the best treatments of the topic, Berry (1980) has proposed that upon contact with a new culture, individuals undergo a process of change in any or all of six areas of psychological functioning: language use, cognitive style, personality, identity, attitudes, and stress. The process of culture learning and change is described by Berry as including an initial stage of crisis or conflict that is then followed by the acceptance of an adaptation strategy. In terms of attitudes, for example, an individual can adapt by assimilation, integration, or rejection of the attitudes prevalent in either culture. In terms of language, Hispanics may completely shift to English, become bilingual, or maintain Spanish as the primary language.

One of the most easily measured changes produced by acculturation takes place in language use, which is probably the reason why it has become a reliable shorthand measure for evaluating acculturation. As a matter of fact, most of the recently published acculturation scales have relied heavily on changes and preferences for language use. Nevertheless, when language used in answering a survey was used alone as a proxy variable for acculturation, about 12% of the respondents were misclassified.

Given the heuristic value of acculturation as an explanation for behavior and attitudinal changes among Hispanics, a number of researchers have published various acculturation scales and indices. Unfortunately, most of them have dealt with only one Hispanic subgroup: Mexican-Americans (Burnam, Telles, Karno, Hough, & Escobar, 1987; Cuellar, Harris, & Jasso, 1980; Deyo, Diehl, Hazuda, & Stern, 1985; Olmedo, Martinez, & Martinez, 1978; Padilla, 1980) or Cubans (Szapocznik & Kurtines, 1980; Szapocznik, Scopetta, Kurtines, & Aranalde, 1978). In addition, few have undergone appropriate psychometric procedures to establish the scale's validity and reliability. One significant problem of many of these acculturation scales is that they have used sociodemographic characteristics (e.g., generation of respondents) as a measurement rather than as a correlate of acculturation. This problem is found in scales where the validation criterion (e.g., generation) is also included as part of the actual scale that is being validated. This decision on the part of researchers produces spuriously high correlations between criterion and scale.

Recently we have published an acculturation scale (Marín, Sabogal, Marín, Otero-Sabogal, & Pérez-Stable, 1987) that can be shortened to four items (all of them dealing with language) and that has shown good psychometric characteristics (see Figure 2.2). That scale has correlated highly with usual validity criteria such as respondents' generation ($r = .69$), length of residence in the United States for foreign-born respondents ($r = .76$), and age at arrival in the United States ($r = -.72$). Its psychometric characteristics, its short length, and the fact that it works equally well with all Hispanic subgroups makes our scale a useful instrument for research with Hispanics. Other short scales that can be utilized to measure Hispanic acculturation are those developed by Burnam et al. (1987), Cuellar et al. (1980), or Szapocznik et al. (1978).

The importance of considering acculturation as a variable that differentiates among subgroups of Hispanics can be seen in the large number of studies that have shown acculturation as a significant modifier of a number of variables. Acculturation levels have been shown to affect among other things Hispanics' mental health status (Szapocznik & Kurtines, 1980); levels of social support (Griffith & Villavicencio, 1985); level of social deviance, alcoholism, and drug use (Graves, 1967; Padilla, Padilla, Ramirez, Morales, & Olmedo, 1979); political and social attitudes (Alva, 1985); and health behaviors such as the consumption of cigarettes (Marín, Pérez-Stable, & Marín, 1989) and the use of preventive cancer screening practices (Marks et al., 1987).

Taking Hispanic Heterogeneity into Consideration

Two important suggestions can be made to solve the dilemma of how to deal with Hispanic heterogeneity. One involves measuring certain core variables that may produce subgroup variations in the dependent variables or in the measures of a study. This core set of variables can include, as a minimum, gender, age, ancestry, amount of formal education, and acculturation level. Investigators would be expected to obtain that information from respondents or informers and to analyze (at least initially) for the possible differences that these so-called independent variables may produce in the results of the investigation. Analyzing by gender, age, and education is something that most social scientists do routinely because those variables are perceived to be central to most social science research. Ancestry and acculturation level, on the other

A. English Version

In general, what language do you read and speak?
    Only Spanish 1
    Spanish better than English 2
    Both equally 3
    English better than Spanish 4
    Only English 5

What language do you usually speak at home?
    Only Spanish 1
    Spanish better than English 2
    Both equally 3
    English better than Spanish 4
    Only English 5

In which language do you usually think?
    Only Spanish 1
    Spanish better than English 2
    Both equally 3
    English better than Spanish 4
    Only English 5

What language do you usually speak with your friends?
    Only Spanish 1
    Spanish better than English 2
    Both equally 3
    English better than Spanish 4
    Only English 5

B. Spanish Version

¿Por lo general, qué idioma(s) lee y habla usted?
    Sólo Español 1
    Más Español qué Inglés 2
    Ambos por igual 3
    Más Inglés qué Español 4
    Sólo Inglés 5

¿Por lo general, qué idioma(s) habla en su casa?
    Sólo Español 1
    Más Español qué Inglés 2
    Ambos por igual 3
    Más Inglés qué Español 4
    Sólo Inglés 5

(continued)

Figure 2.2. Short Accultration Scale

¿Por lo general, en qué idioma(s) piensa?
Sólo Español 1
Más Español qué Inglés 2
Ambos por igual 3
Más Inglés qué Español 4
Sólo Inglés 5

¿Por lo general, qué idioma(s) habla con sus amigos?
Sólo Español 1
Más Español qué Inglés 2
Ambos por igual 3
Más Inglés qué Español 4
Sólo Inglés 5

Figure 2.2. Continued

Scoring instructions: To score, the respondents' answers can be averaged across the four items and the score used as an interval scale, where the scores closer to five indicate high levels of acculturation while those closer to one indicate little acculturation. Alternatively, the respondents' average scores can be split at 2.99 to create a nominal variable. In this case, a score below 2.99 can be considered to reflect low acculturation (less acculturated respondents) while scores above 2.99 would correspond to the more acculturated respondents.

hand, could be expected to be specific to research with ethnic groups. Researchers should note that among Hispanics, acculturation seems to correlate with educational level. In our studies, both variables tend to produce correlation scores of approximately .40. These results imply that when analyzing for acculturation, researchers may need to consider educational level as a covariate.

Similarities in variables of interest across ancestry (i.e., among Mexican-Americans, Cubans, and Puerto Ricans) or across acculturation levels (i.e.., highly acculturated versus the less acculturated) would allow researchers to feel confident in reporting their results for all Hispanics without having to separate findings by ancestry or acculturation level. In some cases, preliminary analyses by acculturation level and ancestry may show the need to separate respondents by these two variables.

Data from one of our studies may serve to show the range of possibilities when this approach is utilized in order to deal with Hispanic heterogeneity. We have found (Marín, Pérez-Stable, & Marín, 1989) that Hispanic men smoke cigarettes in greater proportions (32.4%) than do Hispanic women (16.8%), a pattern that is similar to that found among non-Hispanic Whites (Centers for Disease Control, 1987). Nevertheless, we found that the level of acculturation interacts with gender so that the less acculturated men (37.5%) and the more acculturated

women (22.6%) smoke in greater proportions than the more acculturated men (26.7%) and less acculturated women (13.6%). At the same
time, we found that Mexican-Americans and Central Americans be-
haved in the same fashion in terms of the proportion of men and women
who reported smoking cigarettes.

Another approach involves the development of sampling frames that
are defined a priori and that are based on variables that are assumed to
produce meaningful homogeneous subgroups. This approach emphasizes the need to consider each subpopulation independently and therefore to sample respondents by taking into consideration those variables
that define the subpopulation. One recently proposed scheme within
this approach (Castro & Baezconde-Garbanati, 1987) suggests taking
into consideration four basic variables: migration status (documented
vs. undocumented); personal migration history (U.S.-born vs. immigrant); acculturation level (low, high, or bicultural); and socioeconomic status (low, middle, or high). The crossing of the possible values
of these variables among Hispanics provides for a matrix that has 21
possible different cells. One cell, for example, would be composed
of the low socioeconomic status, low acculturation, U.S.-born, documented respondents while a second cell would be made up of the
low socioeconomic status, high acculturation, U.S.-born, documented
respondents.

Although both of these approaches have some inherently appealing
characteristics, they both share the difficulty of finding specific criteria
to decide on the variables to be considered in the definition of the sample. Arguments can always be presented for one set or another, but
unfortunately there is little evidence to support a particular choice.
Nevertheless, there is one variable that proponents of both approaches
tend to mention: level of acculturation. This is an issue that is relevant in selecting a sample and in interpreting the results (see Chapter 6) and should be included in all studies with Hispanics.

Researchers studying Hispanics should consider the following suggestions on how to deal with Hispanic heterogeneity:

> Investigators need to be aware of the sociodemographic characteristics of
> those Hispanics included in their studies, and the presentation of
> results should include a description of the sample in terms of some
> basic dimensions: gender, age, educational level, socioeconomic sta-
> tus, generation, and acculturation level.
> Ancestry of Hispanic respondents is an essential characteristic to be identi-
> fied among participants in a study. Proportions of each ancestry should

be reported utilizing as a minimum the categories used by the Bureau of the Census: Central Americans, Cubans, Mexican-Americans, Puerto Ricans, South Americans.

In reporting the results of a study that includes collecting data from various respondents or subjects, investigators should first analyze for the effect of some core variables. Of particular importance among Hispanics are ancestry and acculturation level.

Investigators should be careful to avoid overgeneralizing to all Hispanics when the individuals studied belong to a very specific subgroup. For example, generalizing to Hispanics as a whole is inappropriate when respondents were primarily Mexican-Americans.

3

Enhancing Research Participation

A central concern of investigators is being able to access research participants and obtain from them the desired information. This chapter reviews some difficulties usually encountered in accessing and questioning Hispanics and the approaches that facilitate not only the initial contact with the respondents but also accurate completion of the questionnaires and successful follow-up data collection (e.g., panel maintenance in longitudinal studies). The comments included in this chapter will complement those suggestions found in many research methodology books regarding the same topics and many can be applicable to other ethnic or racial minority groups.

ACCESS TO PARTICIPANTS

Hispanics could be expected to be more wary of researchers than are other ethnic or racial groups for a variety of reasons. Primary among these reasons is the concern that providing personal information may place some Hispanics at risk—for example, when income or immigration information could be used against an individual. In addition, some community members perceive social science research as a form of exploitation in which nonminority individuals reap the benefits of the data collection effort (Blauner & Wellman, 1973; Hirsch, 1973; Josephson, 1970; Staples, 1976). Some individuals even advocate that only minority scientists should have access to minority communities (Baca Zinn, 1979; Moore, 1973; Rendon, 1971; Wilson, 1974). These feelings of being exploited or used as guinea pigs could lower participation in a study and negatively affect the quality of the data being collected.

Concerns about participating in research are particularly salient when prospective participants are first contacted in person or over the telephone. It is not uncommon for unscrupulous commercial firms to prey on the newly arrived and convince them to purchase unnecessary or expensive goods at high interest rates. Many times these sales are made under the guise of a contest or a survey and, given their lack of familiarity with such procedures, unsuspecting and naive individuals are often deceived by these gimmicks. Once these strategies are known in a community, word of mouth spreads the message that there is a need to be wary of strangers asking questions. Suspicion of government involvement in a research project is more likely when individuals or their family members and friends have lived in political climates where oppressive governments make use of informers and home visits to gather compromising information to be used in surveillance, social control, or other abuses of a person's rights. In addition, many Hispanics, regardless of their immigration status (documented, undocumented, refugee, parolee), live in fear of being stopped by agents of the Immigration and Naturalization Service and of being asked to document their citizenship or immigration status.

Given this justifiable wariness, it is surprising that researchers generally have found that Hispanics are willing and interested participants in research endeavors, irrespective of the sampling approach or the type of research project. Analyses of survey data (e.g., Marín, Pérez-Stable & Marín, 1989) show that Hispanic respondents can be contacted with ease in person or by telephone. More important, various studies have shown that Hispanics often agree to participate in surveys in proportions that are higher than those usually found among non-Hispanic Whites. In the Marín, Pérez-Stable, and Marín (1989) study, two large-scale telephone surveys of Hispanics were conducted and refusal rates were quite low (4.7% and 3.1%). Comparable studies that involve non-Hispanic Whites report refusal rates between 20% and 25% (Frey, 1983). High response rates for surveys with Hispanics have also been reported by other researchers conducting studies on topics as varied as health services and needs (Aday, Chiu, & Andersen, 1980), media use patterns (Shoemaker, Reese, & Danielson, 1985), migrant workers' experiences (Zusman & Olson, 1977), political attitudes (Freeman, 1969), illegal drug use (Ball & Pabon, 1965), and the evaluation of mental health services (Burgoyne, Wolkon, & Staples, 1977).

Various explanations may be given for this unusual willingness to cooperate with investigators. One is that basic cultural factors such as the *simpatía* social script (Triandis, Marín, Lisansky, & Betancourt, 1984) in Hispanic culture promote fluid, positive, and cooperative social relations. A second possibility is that Hispanics may have a true altruistic desire to cooperate in research activities that benefit the community as a whole or other Hispanics in particular. A third possibility is that, in general, Hispanics have not been studied with the same intensity as other ethnic or racial groups who in the process have developed negative reactions to the intrusiveness of researchers. Whatever explanation is true, the fact remains that for the most part Hispanics are cooperative participants in research endeavors that promise some social good as an outcome. While this general disposition makes the job of researchers easier, it also imposes special responsibilities on the part of investigators to collect high quality data in an appropriate manner.

There are of course, factors that temper Hispanics' overall interest in cooperating with researchers. One is the extent of the demands that the research project places on the individual. These include aspects such as the length of the research procedures (e.g., time required to answer an interview); the type of physical effort required (e.g., drawing blood or writing for long periods of time); and the environmental requirements of the study (e.g., lengthy travel to the research site or interruptions during family meals). As with any ethnic group, the greater the demands placed on the respondents, the lower the likelihood that full cooperation will be obtained.

Another aspect of a research project that may affect Hispanics' interest in participating is the type of issue or topic being researched. Cooperation with a survey, for example, can be expected to differ if the topic deals with general attitudes toward recycling or with information about the respondents' sexual practices. The lower level of self-disclosure to strangers, particularly among Hispanic men, that has been documented by some researchers (Franco, Malloy, & Gonzalez, 1984; LeVine & Franco, 1981; Levine & Padilla, 1980) is an important factor in the degree of overall cooperation that may be expected from research participants. If Hispanics are indeed less prone to self-disclose to strangers, one can expect that fewer potential respondents will agree to participate in a study and that the quality of the data may be impaired by the fact that details may be left out or behaviors not accurately reported.

Also of relevance in determining the rate of cooperation with an investigation is the type of personal or community benefit that is to be accrued by participating in the study. Clearly perceived community benefits to be derived from the data or compensation to the participants in terms of money or services rendered, will often enhance the level of participation.

Subject selection, particularly in survey research (Henry, 1990), is one research procedure that can be expected to be seriously affected by the issues mentioned above. Because many traditional approaches to respondent selection require the enumeration of all household residents, concerns about the legitimacy of a study, among other factors, may hinder the accuracy of the responses provided and the representativeness of the sample surveyed. Recently, various authors have suggested that the complicated enumeration of all household residents (usually known as the Kish method) is not essential for producing a truly random sample (O'Rourke & Blair, 1983; Salmon & Nichols, 1983). Alternative methods include the alternation between males and females, the interviewing of the household resident with the most recent or the next birthday, and the production of selection matrices that take into account various demographic characteristics of interest such as age and gender (the Troldahl-Carter method). Our experiences with Hispanics have shown that the last birthday method is perceived as noninvasive by Hispanic residents and it has produced a minimal number of refusals although, as shown with non-minority respondents, there is tendency for more females than males to be part of the final sample. In this method, interviewers ask to speak to the respondent who had the most recent birthday and whose age falls within the parameters of interest in the study.

A number of strategies have been utilized in the past to optimize collaboration with a research project. First, researchers must become thoroughly familiar with the community to be studied in terms of its sociodemographic characteristics, needs, information channels, power structures, and the like. Second, investigators must be able to establish the ethical integrity and scientific and professional legitimacy of their study to anyone who may question it. These issues are discussed in greater detail below.

Becoming Familiar With the Community

Successfully accessing Hispanic research participants demands an understanding of demographic information about Hispanics in general and, in particular, about the communities in which they live that at times is not easily available. This information is useful both in contacting potential respondents as well as in obtaining community support for a given research project or data collection effort. Often this information on Hispanics is deficient or lacking due to outdated statistics (e.g., the decennial census reports) or to the lack of prior research in a specialized area (e.g., information on sexual behavior patterns). In designing sampling strategies, the work of ethnographers (Fetterman, 1989; Jorgensen, 1989) and other social scientists can complement official statistics that may be available through local or federal government agencies such as the Bureau of the Census or county health offices. Also useful in understanding the makeup of a community is information from local leaders who may be able to provide valuable insights into the demographic characteristics of an area of a city or information on important characteristics of a community. Among the information that may be useful in this respect are the names of places often frequented by Hispanics, preferred shopping and recreational areas, names of adult education programs, and names of social and community organizations serving Hispanics.

Establishing Legitimacy

The investigator must demonstrate sufficient legitimacy to allay fears that the information being collected will be misused, that the research project is a gimmick used by commercial enterprises to sell products, or that the government is trying to obtain information about the respondents—possibly to check their immigration status. Properly established legitimacy on the part of the researcher will in many cases eliminate or reduce the misgivings of participants about the ultimate reason for a given study.

Legitimacy can be enhanced if initial contacts are carried out by bilingual Hispanic researchers or interviewers who are more likely to be seen as part of the community and not personally threatening. In face-to-face contacts, attention should be given to such status legitimization components as researchers dressing well but not luxuriously, wearing an identification badge, and carrying letters and other documents proving the connection of the project with legitimate local institutions such as clinics, schools, or churches.

Special attention also should be given to the scripting of the initial message to be presented to the potential research participant. This message should be personal (i.e., include the name of the researcher or interviewer), mention the purpose of the study, explicitly include the legitimizing agency (e.g., local university), summarize what is expected of the participants in the study, and make known the amount of any compensation involved. If the initial contact is made over the telephone, the name of the legitimizing agency should be part of the initial sentence (e.g., "Hello, my name is Carlos and I am calling from State University . . . ") Details also should be included regarding the way in which the telephone number was chosen so as to lower the anxiety produced when a stranger calls.

The above suggestions are usually sufficient for small-scale studies or research projects that demand little effort on the part of the participant. Studies that make significant demands on the respondent (e.g., providing blood samples, answering highly personal questions, submitting to lengthy interviews or to physical exams) require additional steps to ensure access to respondents. Examples of these studies include projects such as the H-HANES or clinical studies designed to identify prevalence and incidence of serious illnesses or conditions (e.g., depression, tuberculosis, infection with HIV). Because of the characteristics of these studies, researchers should implement the additional procedures detailed in the following sections on community consultation, community sponsorship, and informing the community.

Community Consultation

The issue of community consultation should be of particular concern to field researchers or those carrying out research in community settings (Bengston, Grigsby, Corry, & Hruby, 1977; Humm-Delgado & Delgado, 1985). Ideally, this consultation should begin during the planning stage of the study and should continue through the analysis, interpretation, and publication of the data. Early consultation can prevent problems that may arise from improper instrumentation, inclusion of sensitive topics that may bias the results or produce high refusal or break-off rates, or difficulties in accessing specific respondents. At a minimum, community consultation may provide the researcher access to respondents and may substantially benefit the design of the study.

The process of involving the community in the design of a study can take the form of public forums or the use of key informants or consultants (Humm-Delgado & Delgado, 1985). In a public forum, the researchers present to community members the plans for the study and answer any questions they may have. These forums can be specially programmed and advertised and held in schools, theaters, or churches located in the community that is going to be studied. Another option for the forums would be to visit meetings of large community associations (e.g., social clubs, fraternal groups, churches) and present the study as part of their regularly scheduled meeting. The choice of options will depend, of course, on the time available and the extent of the need for community consultation.

Key informants or consultants can serve functions similar to those of community forums in that they can give feedback to the researchers on their plans and inform prospective participants of the upcoming study.

These individuals can be found as staff, members, or clients of educational institutions, community service agencies, churches and temples, and voluntary associations. In many cases, in a "snowball" approach, a community leader provides a list of other leaders who in turn provide additional names. This process will easily generate a fairly large list of prospective community consultants.

In many cases, a subgroup of the individuals who have served as key informants and consultants can be invited to serve on an advisory board. This board can help researchers to assess properly the needs of the community as these change during the life of the project. Furthermore, an advisory board can help in the design of instruments and in other aspects of the research project by sharing with the researchers their knowledge of and experiences with the community. The existence of an advisory board can also enhance the participation of community members by opening doors that otherwise might remain closed.

In seeking community consultation, the level of involvement that the community, the consultants, or the advisory board will have in designing and implementing the study should be clearly specified. Clarity in this sensitive topic will prevent future problems of unmet expectations. In addition, experiences in various studies (e.g., Bengston et al., 1977) involving community consultation have shown that the researchers need to be flexible in their plans in order to accommodate community requests and concerns that in some cases may necessitate substantial revisions of the original research protocol.

Obtaining Community Sponsorship

An additional strategy utilized by some researchers to obtain access to minority participants is to obtain the sponsorship of a community leader or organization. When this is done, the research can be presented to the respondents as being sanctioned by the sponsoring individuals or institutions. Zusman and Olson (1977), for example, were able to obtain lengthy interviews from Hispanic migrant workers when the study was sponsored by their crew leaders.

This approach is particularly useful among individuals who mistrust non-Hispanic organizations or researchers or are uncertain about their intentions. Studies that require the participants to divulge many details about their lives (e.g., anthropological studies) or sensitive information about themselves (e.g., sexual behavior, income) can in particular benefit from such sponsorship. Cooperation can be obtained more easily when a study or an interview has the sponsorship of individuals or institutions that in the past have shown concern for the welfare of the members of the community.

A possible negative side effect of sponsorship is that it depends entirely on the name recognition and favorable image that the sponsoring institution or individual has in the community. While this approach may open some doors it also may close those of individuals who are unaware of the existence of the sponsoring organization or who mistrust or dislike the community organization or leader. Since some rivalry is common in all communities, the researcher who wishes to obtain community sponsorship should become familiar with community members' perceptions of the sponsoring body. An alternative is to obtain the sponsorship of various community leaders and organizations so that if some respondents distrust one agency there may be other agencies on the list that they trust.

Informing the Community About the Study

One important concern in large-scale studies is providing sufficient information to the community about the characteristics of the study, its sponsorship, the usefulness of the data, and other pertinent details. This information will facilitate the collaboration of community members and enhance the chances of success on the initial contact between researcher or interviewer and prospective participants. Ideally, details on large-scale community studies should be communicated through as many channels as possible, including personal letters to potential participants and messages in the electronic and printed media. In preparing this information attention should be given to addressing properly the concerns of the prospective participants and to providing sufficient legitimizing information regarding the study and its sponsoring institutions.

Besides informing potential participants of the fact that the study is going to be carried out, informational messages on the study can also provide motivational arguments to enhance participation. In preparation for the H-HANES for example, well-known artists were contracted to film television public service announcements describing the study and the benefits it would bring to the community. In addition, Spanish-speaking health personnel participated in talk shows to explain the need for the study, its expected benefits, and what would be required of those invited to participate. Posters and flyers also carried the same messages. Other very demanding studies (e.g., those requiring respondents to provide blood samples and to answer highly personal questions) have relied on letters sent to the residences of potential respondents ahead of the initial enumeration contact. These letters have the advantage of minimizing the reaction of surprise of prospective participants when first contacted by an interviewer. The letters are also useful in creating legitimacy for the study since they are usually written on official letterhead and may include copies of letters of support of well-known community leaders.

The choice of media utilized in advertising the research project should reflect the use patterns of the targeted community. The messages should be carefully pretested to ensure that they address the community's concerns in a culturally appropriate fashion. Even a proper translation into Spanish or the hiring of a Hispanic scriptwriter does not guarantee a culturally appropriate message. Attention needs to be given to the community's expectations, attitudes, and values regarding the study or the topic of the research project. In many cases, these issues are culture-specific or group-specific and will need to be properly identified before the messages are produced (see Chapter 4).

In summary, two strategies should be used by all researchers who attempt to gain access to Hispanic respondents:

Become well informed about the local community. This implies going beyond census data and obtaining the type of information that will help the researcher better understand the way in which a community functions.

Establish legitimacy through documented sponsorship as well as by careful dress and demeanor of interviewers.

In addition, researchers planning to carry out large-scale studies may consider implementing the following suggestions in order to enhance participation:

Knowledgeable members of the community should be consulted in order to obtain information on issues of concern to the respondents, approaches to be used to announce the study properly, procedures that can be implemented to enhance participation, and methods for informing the community of the results of the study.

Community sponsorship may be sought from institutions or individuals who support the research effort. A careful analysis should be initially conducted to identify the power structures, both formal and informal, of the community.

The media should be used to inform and motivate the community about the study.

If possible, letters should be sent to the members of the population to be sampled announcing the study and the approximate date on which they will be contacted. These letters should be printed on the official letterhead of a respected local institution. If available, the support of well-respected local authorities may be mentioned (e.g., city's bishop, mayor).

Those collecting data or asking questions should carry with them copies of the letters sent to the respondents announcing the study as well as originals of letters introducing them as staff members of the study. Official letterhead should again be used.

ENHANCING COMPLETION OF
RESEARCH PROTOCOLS

Some early researchers in largely unpublished reports have suggested that Hispanics are more likely than other groups to fail to complete research protocols. In many cases, those early research projects were insensitive to many of the issues raised in this book. In addition, other studies have encountered difficulties following individuals who migrate yearly from job to job throughout the United States (e.g., Welch, Comer, & Steinman, 1973). Nevertheless, a significant number of recent studies have shown not only very low refusal rates among Hispanics (Freeman, 1969; Grebler et al., 1970; Marín, Pérez-Stable & Marín, 1989; Welch et al., 1973; Zusman & Olson, 1977) but also higher completion rates for Hispanics than for non-Hispanic Whites (Burgoyne et al., 1977; Zusman & Olson, 1977).

Lack of attention to certain aspects of the design and implementation of a research protocol is often responsible for the difficulties experienced in obtaining cooperation from the intended participants. These difficulties when experienced as part of a study will negatively affect the quality of the data collected. Researchers interested in enhancing Hispanics' level of cooperation need to pay special attention to such aspects as language appropriateness of the protocols, the ethnicity of the members of the research team, and the type of instrument to be utilized in data collection. These issues are reviewed below.

Language

One aspect of a research project that may affect the rate of completion among Hispanic respondents is the linguistic appropriateness of the interaction between researchers or interviewers and the participants. Chapters 4 and 5 deal with approaches to be used in ensuring that the instruments properly reflect the culture and the linguistic needs of the research participants. The concern here is with choosing the appropriate language for conducting the interview.

Identifying the preferred language of the research participants can be accomplished by simply asking respondents which language they prefer to use when participating in the study. In our communitywide telephone surveys we have used a simple question at the beginning of the interview in order to ascertain preferred language ("I can ask you these questions in Spanish or in English. Which language do you prefer?"). Overall, close to 70% of San Francisco Hispanics have preferred to use Spanish rather than English. It is interesting to note that in our communitywide surveys we have found a significant proportion of highly acculturated Hispanics (23.2%) who prefer to answer a questionnaire in Spanish rather than in English.

When contacting possible respondents over the telephone, attention should be paid to the language used in answering the call. If Spanish is used (e.g., "Ola," "¿Aló?," "¿Díga?," "¿Oigo?,") the conversation should be initiated in Spanish, even before the language preference question is asked.

As could be expected from a vibrant language, there are variations in the way Spanish is used (primarily in terms of preferred vocabulary) that are closely related to geographical regions. In an early study (Ryan & Carranza, 1976) standard Spanish was viewed as more appropriate than regional variations. The inclusion of parochial wording in instrument translation is a highly sensitive issue covered more completely in Chapter 5 but it deserves mention here. Unless participants are known ahead of time to have problems dealing with standard Spanish, instruments, instructions, and any other communication should be prepared in the type of Spanish that is universally understood, the type of Spanish utilized by radio and television networks in the United States. This standard Spanish or "broadcast Spanish" is free of regional or national variations and utilizes standard terms to refer to those nouns that change from country to country. Whenever regional variations are present and very salient (e.g., names of certain fruits, technological discoveries), researchers should use all possible variations in the same sentence (e.g., in talking about oranges, the Spanish word "*naranja*" should be used; but if Puerto Ricans are to be sampled, "*china*" should be added to "*naranja*").

To increase respondent collaboration, care should be taken in training researchers or interviewers to address potential participants with respect. Special attention should be given to the use of the two pronouns for "you" in Spanish (the informal "*tu*" and the formal and respectful "*usted*"). Except when talking to adolescents and children, interviewers should use the formal pronoun (*usted*). Among certain Caribbean respondents (e.g., Cuba, Puerto Rico, Dominican Republic) the informal *tu* may be appropriate, but researchers should wait for the respondent to initiate its use.

Ethnicity of Members of the Research Team

A related issue to consider when trying to enhance participation in a study is the ethnicity of the individuals charged with data collection. This is of particular concern in studies involving interviewing or other verbal approaches to data collection where personal contact is usually established with the participant and where certain nuances or subtleties may be lost to those unfamiliar with the culture. Of equal importance is the need to include minority individuals as members of the research team as investigators or consultants to the researchers carrying out the study.

Interviewers or data gatherers. Various researchers (e.g., Bloom & Padilla, 1979) have suggested that same-ethnicity data collectors should be employed in research projects where personal contact is involved. Interviewers or researchers of the same ethnicity as the respondents can enhance rapport, willingness to disclose, and the validity and reliability of the data provided. Similarities in background can enhance participants' trust of the research team and, in this fashion, motivate them not only to complete the research process but also to provide accurate information (Bloom & Padilla, 1979). Being ethnically similar to the interviewer can help the participants feel that they share experiences with the members of the project. This can be of particular importance in methodologies where the collection of information is heavily dependent on establishing good rapport between researcher and participant, as is the case in studies utilizing participant observations (Jorgensen, 1989) or open-ended questions. As a matter of fact, Bernal, North, Rosen, Delfini, and Schultz (1979) found that when Mexican-American children were observed at home by non-Hispanic

Whites, they were more nonverbally abusive and less compliant than when the observations were made by Mexican-Americans, although the differences were not statistically significant.

Although there are few studies with Hispanics, the bulk of studies with African-Americans show that there is an interviewer effect so that the race of the interviewer affects the type of data provided by the research participants, particularly when the issues are perceived as sensitive or highly personal. In a recent study, for example, Anderson, Silver, and Abramson (1988) found that when African-Americans were interviewed by non-Hispanic Whites, they were more likely to express warmth and closeness toward Whites than when African-Americans were interviewed by individuals of their own race. In another study looking at national representative samples, Schaeffer (1980) found that the responses given by African-Americans tended to vary according to the race of the interviewer. Furthermore, a study by Cotter (1982) found that this race-of-interviewer effect occurred not only when respondents were interviewed face to face but also when questionnaires were filled out in front of the interviewer and when surveys were conducted over the telephone.

Nevertheless, there are findings that show that the accuracy of the responses provided by ethnic minorities to nonsensitive questions is not impaired by utilizing interviewers that belong to an ethnic or racial group different from that of the respondents (Weeks & Moore, 1981). The use of same-ethnicity interviewers may produce better rapport, as suggested by Bloom and Padilla (1979), although the quality of the data when asking nonsensitive questions may not be affected.

Researchers. Good arguments also exist for the inclusion of Hispanic researchers as part of the research team. Nonminority researchers or even researchers who do not belong to the ethnic group being studied often have difficulties understanding the realities of a cultural group that is different from their own (Moore, 1973; Rogler, Malgady, & Rodriguez, 1989; Wilson, 1974). Some researchers (Garcia, 1972; Good & Good, 1986) for example, have argued that a substantial proportion of the differences in results found between Hispanics and non-Hispanics in epidemiological studies of psychopathology can be explained in part by differences of interpretation by professionals unacquainted with Hispanic culture and by biased psychological instruments. Good and Good (1986) cite data showing that as many as 75% of Hispanic mental patients may have been misdiagnosed by non-Hispanic therapists. Because of their shared experiences and culture, minority researchers may be better qualified to properly analyze and understand a given phenomenon among minority communities. The participation of minority researchers can enhance the quality of a study by contributing their culture-specific knowledge of the behavior or issue to be studied. Such knowledge can lead to the inclusion of topics, constructs, and variables that would otherwise be ignored by nonminority researchers. In addition, minority researchers can bring an insider's understanding of the research topic from the community's own particular perspective, contributing in this fashion to the better interpretation of the results of the study.

Merton (1972) has suggested that both perspectives (minority and nonminority) need to be included in a study in order to understand reality more properly. The involvement of minority researchers in key decision-making roles seems essential to provide input into the design of the project, the choice of instrumentation, and the interpretation and use of the data (Moore, 1973). Genuine collaboration between minority and nonminority researchers can only enhance the validity of the data and their future usefulness to both science and the community being studied.

Often the argument is presented that there are few minority researchers available or that research budgets do not allow the inclusion of large staffs. The last few years have seen a significant increase in the number of minority professionals in the various social and behavioral sciences thanks to active recruitment efforts of minority graduate students by various universities. Most professional associations now have a division or an office dedicated to ethnic minority affairs and these offices can be contacted for leads on how to identify minority researchers interested in a given topic who might want to participate in a research project. Recent efforts on the part of the National Institutes of Health (NIH) and of the Alcohol, Drug Abuse and Mental Health Administration (ADAMHA) make it possible for researchers to request additional funds to pay for the salary of minority researchers. These funds are usually provided as additions to the parent grant and, by increasing the research staff, these grants can enormously benefit the outcome of the study. These funding initiatives are called Minority Research Initiatives within NIH and Supplements for Underrepresented Minorities in Biomedical and Behavioral Research within ADAMHA. Information on requirements and application procedures can be obtained from any program officer at these institutes.

Compensation for Participation

A third consideration regarding increased participation involves providing participants with appropriate compensation for their efforts. Many studies place limited burdens on their participants (e.g., answering questions for 10 minutes over the telephone) while other studies demand large investments of time and effort (e.g., a 2-hour long interview, performance of various physical tasks, disclosure of highly personal information). In these latter cases, research participants should be compensated for their efforts. Compensation can take the form of services provided (e.g., free medical examinations); enhancement of the community's environment (e.g., free books or subscription to a magazine; donations of toys or minor appliances); or, more commonly, monetary rewards.

Researchers with little experience working with minorities and low-income groups usually express concern that providing compensation to research participants will vitiate the quality of the data because of a self-selection bias. There is little or no evidence for these concerns. What can be asserted is that the usual demands of a research interview are often more burdensome for minority group members. Because of their generally low socioeconomic status, many minority individuals may work more hours than nonminority persons, work two jobs, or have more difficult home situations (more children to care for, fewer economic resources, fewer labor saving devices). These circumstances make it a greater burden on the average for a minority individual to spend 15 minutes answering a questionnaire than for a nonminority respondent. The limited educational attainment also more common to some minority group members often places an additional burden when the individuals are asked to complete questionnaires or respond to complicated scales. Thus monetary rewards or other incentives are not only useful but also appropriate for minority participants.

A question remains as to the actual amount of the compensation. The individual should be compensated for time spent at a relevant hourly rate. If additional expenses are involved (e.g., transportation costs), these also should be reimbursed. If special demands are placed on the individual (e.g., disclosure of sensitive information) the amount of compensation should be higher. Nevertheless, care should be taken that the compensation offered does not exceed what is appropriate so that it does not appear that the individual is being bribed into participating in the study. The proper amount to be offered research participants before the compensation becomes a bribe is difficult to estimate since any amount may be perceived as a bribe to an unemployed person. Community consultation can be an excellent source of information in this regard.

Instrument Format

It is likely that poorly educated individuals may find it difficult to deal with written materials, especially complex response scales or multiple-choice questions. Therefore researchers must become fully aware of the educational characteristics of the population to be studied. Census data and other communitywide surveys may provide essential information on average level of education of the members of the community, levels of functional illiteracy, and so on.

Among Hispanics, statistics on literacy and school achievement vary significantly from group to group and from region to region. As noted in Chapter 1, the various Hispanic subgroups differ in their median level of education, with Mexican-Americans being the lowest. Furthermore, even in urban areas it is still possible to find a number of individuals who have not received any type of formal education. Our surveys show that approximately 2% of San Francisco's Hispanics have failed to complete at least one year of formal education (Marín, Pérez-Stable, & Marín, 1989).

The linguistic and educational characteristics of a population are just two aspects that need to be taken into consideration when designing the instruments to be utilized in a given study. It is most important that participants have adequate knowledge to utilize the response formats used in the instrument. Researchers should not assume that recently migrated ethnic minorities will be able to properly manage scaling approaches such as those commonly used in survey research (e.g., Likert-type scales) without proper training. This training can be as simple as asking respondents to think of a simple event such as eating breakfast and showing them how to use the response scale (e.g., "If you never eat breakfast, then mark the box with the number 1 that says Never; if you eat breakfast every single day, then mark the box with the number 5 that says Always"). Once respondents are provided with appropriate training, even poorly educated individuals can respond utilizing four- and five-point scales over the telephone or in person (e.g., Marín, Sabogal, Marín, Otero-Sabogal, & Pérez-Stable, 1987).

Projective techniques may be especially inappropriate for use with non-English-speaking or poorly educated groups. Interpretation of responses to projective techniques is based solely upon subtle linguistic variations requiring complete awareness on the part of the researcher of the connotative and denotative meaning of words. Certain environmental circumstances (e.g., level and type of education; experience with manual labor) may affect the choice of words in a given language (Brislin, Lonner, & Thorndike, 1973; Lindzey, 1961) and the interpretation that may be made of the responses. The use of projective techniques creates special difficulties with Hispanics when poorly educated and less verbal respondents are studied, when researchers are not fully conversant with the language used by the participants, or when the individuals being studied prefer to use regional forms of Spanish or mixtures of English and Spanish. Furthermore, certain Hispanics (e.g., poorly educated rural residents, recent immigrants from rural areas in Latin America) may perceive the pictorial stimuli in ways that are quite different from the experiences of other Hispanics more familiar with the environment in which most projective techniques have been developed. These differential experiences may produce responses to projective stimuli that are not comparable across Hispanic subgroups, much less across ethnic groups (Marín, 1986).

Type of Data Collection Approach

Most studies that utilize surveys in the social sciences (Fowler, 1988) make use of one of four basic data collection approaches: face-to-face interviews in which respondents verbalize their answers to the interviewer; face-to-face interviews in which the participants write down their answers; telephone interviews; and self-administered paper-and-pencil instruments. Various researchers have expressed concerns about the validity and appropriateness of these methods when doing research with Hispanics (e.g., Aday et al., 1980; Howard et al., 1983; Welch et al., 1973) although little is known about the possible effect of the research approach on refusal and completion rates.

The type of data collection approach chosen is particularly significant when the study deals with sensitive or highly personal topics (e.g., drug use, sexual behavior, immigration). Given that the usual survey approaches vary in terms of their intrusiveness and consequent discomfort or embarrassment to the respondent, completion rates and response accuracy may be affected. A recent study found that Hispanics tend to provide inconsistent answers and to underreport when surveyed about illegal, deviant, or non-normative behavior (Mensch & Kandel, 1988).

In a methodological study (Marín & Marín, 1989) we compared three interviewing approaches (face-to-face with respondents verbalizing responses to interviewer; face-to-face with respondents writing down their answers in private; and telephone interviews) to assess refusal and completion rates, the perceived discomfort of the interviewee when answering highly sensitive questions (e.g., drug use, sexual preferences, patterns of sexual behavior), as well as the perceived accuracy of the responses that interviewees would provide in these types of surveys. The respondents were 217 randomly selected adult Hispanics in San Francisco. The results showed that there were no differences among interviewing approaches in the number of individuals who refused to participate in the study, although 7% of those interviewed over the telephone chose to discontinue the interview before completion compared with none of those interviewed face to face. The proportion of respondents leaving questions unanswered did not differ across survey approaches. Furthermore, respondents reported feeling equally comfortable answering the highly personal questions in any of the interviewing approaches but telephone surveys were perceived to produce more truthful responses when very personal topics such as type and gender of sexual partner were discussed. The above study shows that the data collection approach may affect the level of cooperation and the quality of the data obtained in a survey with Hispanics.

As could be expected, telephone interviews may increase the rates of discontinued participation—it is easier to hang up on interviewers than to ask them to leave one's home. However, respondents may be more willing to tell the truth and therefore to provide more accurate results in a telephone survey than when being interviewed face to face (Marín, Pérez-Stable, & Marín, 1989; Portes & Bach, 1985).

Recently, we have found that telephone interviews with Hispanics are feasible, more economical than face-to-face interviews, and show low refusal rates (Marín, Marín, & Pérez-Stable, 1990). We have modified the Mitofsky-Waksberg (Waksberg, 1978) random-digit-dialing procedure to maximize the possibilities of encountering Hispanic households, while still avoiding the biases introduced by sampling from telephone directories. As part of the sampling procedure we have identified three-digit telephone prefixes that are usually assigned to census tracts with high concentrations of Hispanics (over 10%). These three-digit prefixes are then assigned randomly selected four-digit suffixes to make up the telephone numbers to be called. Following Waksberg's suggestions, whenever one of these numbers produces a

Hispanic household, the first five digits are saved to form the Primary Sampling Unit.

In surveys of smoking behavior, alcohol use, awareness of health promotion messages, and AIDS prevention among San Francisco Hispanics, we found low refusal rates (consistently below 10%) and high response rates, even without advance publicity of the study. Other researchers (Shoemaker et al., 1985) also report low refusal rates with Hispanics in Texas. Researchers who intend to use random-digit-dialing methods should first identify the percentage of Hispanic households with telephones, since this varies widely in different areas. The 1980 census figures indicate that 92% of Hispanic households in San Francisco had a telephone, compared to 74% of Hispanic households in New York (Adams-Esquivel & Lang, 1987).

In summary, the following suggestions can enhance continued participation in a study:

All interactions with ethnic minority research participants should be conducted in the language of their choice. Instruments and research protocols should be available in the languages used by the respondents (English and Spanish for Hispanics). In addition, research personnel having contact with participants should be fully fluent in the preferred languages of the individuals.

The use of same-ethnicity research personnel (interviewers, experimenters, observers, etc.) will enhance the quality of the data and the rates of participation in the study.

Minority research participants should be compensated for their efforts in proportion to the demands placed on them by the researchers.

Instruments that utilize complex scaling techniques or response categories that may be unfamiliar to less educated respondents should be carefully pretested and properly explained to respondents.

In collecting survey data, the usual approaches seem to be equally useful and appropriate with Hispanics. Telephone interviews are not only more economical but may provide more valid responses, especially when the survey deals with sensitive or highly personal topics.

ENSURING CONTINUED OR LONG-TERM CONTACT WITH SUBJECTS

Some researchers need to contact research participants repeatedly. Some studies call for contacting participants at intervals of weeks, months, and even years. Little is known about difficulties inherent in following up Hispanic participants although some studies have been able to recontact a substantial proportion of individuals after one or more years.

Longitudinal research approaches could present particular problems when studying Hispanics given the high mobility rate of the recently migrated and the high proportion of individuals who rent rather than own their place of residence. Our experiences in San Francisco (Marín, Marín, Pérez-Stable, Otero-Sabogal, & Sabogal, 1990) indicate that it is possible to recontact 87% of Hispanics interviewed on the street 30 days after the initial interview. In that case, respondents only provided their name, address, and home telephone number. Nevertheless, we have experienced attrition rates as high as 45% among urban Hispanics who are recontacted 12 months after the initial survey. Another study with Hispanics in semirural areas of Texas has reported an average rate of 65% recontacts two years after the initial interview (McAlister et al., in press).

Traditional approaches to maintaining contact with research participants across time (panel maintenance) involve obtaining the names of relatives or friends who would know the whereabouts of the research participants. If during follow-up a research participant is not found at home or by telephone as logged in the initial research protocols, the researchers can contact their friends, relatives, or their place of employment to obtain the current address or telephone number of the respondents. This procedure is based on the assumptions that when people move they do not cut off their ties with friends, relatives, and work associates and that these individuals would be willing to assist the researchers in contacting the research participant.

The above approaches are useful with Hispanics and should be implemented as the minimum steps in guaranteeing panel maintenance. Recently, Portes and Bach (1985) have used some of the above suggestions in trying to follow up recently migrated Hispanics and have obtained a significant measure of success. In their study of Cuban and Mexican immigrants, Portes and Bach were able to reinterview approximately 72% of the original Cuban sample 3 years after the first contact and 70% after 6 years. Their experiences with Mexican immigrants were somewhat different since approximately 53% were recontacted after 3 years and 55% after 6 years of the initial interview. The respondents in that study were asked to provide the names and addresses of two friends or relatives and their place of employment together with their intended place of residence (for those just entering the United

States). The difference in follow-up rates for Cuban and Mexican immigrants is probably due to the fact that the Cubans tended to remain in Miami, Florida, while the Mexicans moved to different places in the country. Because Cuban immigrants for the most part remained in one geographical area it was easier to find the respondents through the reference persons and through places of employment.

An obvious difficulty with these traditional methods of panel maintenance is the reluctance of certain individuals to provide names and addresses for themselves and for their friends and relatives. In our studies we have found that approximately 10% of Hispanic respondents refuse to provide this information compared with 29% of non-Hispanic Whites.

Other ways of insuring panel maintenance that researchers may wish to consider are (a) postage-paid postcards that participants mail back to inform researchers of address or telephone changes; (b) participation certificates or membership cards including a request to inform the researchers of changes in domicile; (c) greeting cards sent at certain times of the year (e.g., Christmas, Easter, Hispanic Heritage Month) including a request to the Postal Service for change of address information (this service is provided for a small fee if requested on the front of the envelope); and (d) periodic payments or incentives given to the respondents, with a higher incentive being promised for participation in the last data-gathering opportunity. Newsletters also can serve to maintain contact with research participants without becoming too obtrusive. It may also be useful to call or visit research participants regularly and, if they have moved, to ask neighbors or current residents for forwarding addresses and telephone numbers.

If a respondent is lost to the study, several tracking strategies may be useful. If the survey is being conducted over the telephone and the number is reported as disconnected by the telephone company, the researcher may wish to recontact the same number the following month since a large proportion of telephone numbers are disconnected due to lack of payment rather than change of residence. Once payment is made, the telephone service is reinstated and the original respondent can once again be contacted. In our attempts to follow up respondents over a 12-month period we found a significant proportion of telephones reported as disconnected that were once again operational within a month's time and still belonged to the study participants.

Lost respondents can also be tracked by checking for new telephone numbers through the directory assistance services of the various telephone companies. Several additional sources of information about a person's current address exist: (a) Neighbors of the respondent at the original address may know their new address. Telephone numbers of neighbors can be obtained in a street directory, a reverse directory that lists telephone numbers by address. These directories are available from telephone companies or from commercial vendors. (b) Social service agencies (county and state) may have records of having helped a particular individual. (c) Individuals with the same last name listed in the telephone directory for the last known place of residence of the respondents may be relatives of the participants. (d) School districts or schools serving the area where the respondents lived most recently may have a forwarding address or may forward a letter to the respondents, depending on the privacy legislation in effect in a given state. (e) Churches serving the last known area of residence of the respondents may have forwarding addresses or names and addresses of respondents' friends.

Certain individuals may be found through the Veterans Administration (if they have served in the armed forces); the county's voter registration rolls (if they are citizens and they have registered to vote); death registries; the state departments that issue driver's licenses and car registrations (if they drive or own a car); or penitentiaries (Bindman, Lurie, and Wenger, personal communication, 1989). These sources of information are more difficult to use, may help locate only individuals who have particular characteristics (e.g., who drive or vote), and may require information about the respondent that researchers may not have access to, such as social security numbers or driver's license numbers.

The above procedures can of course be utilized with any type of respondent regardless of his or her ethnicity. There are some additional steps that can be taken to enhance the possibilities of recontacting ethnic minority research participants at follow-up. One possibility for recontacting recently migrated Hispanics is to visit the consulate of their country of origin for information on their most recent address. Many countries require their citizens to register with their consulate upon arrival in a foreign country. Others keep records of their citizens who have visited the consulate for such matters as passport renewals, income tax filing, issuing of citizenship cards, or military service deferments. An additional step, especially in large metropolitan areas, is to contact the social welfare associations that serve individuals from one specific country. The respondents may continue to be members of these associations, or association officers may know the current addresses of former members.

It is also feasible to place announcements in ethnic media (radio or newspapers) indicating the researchers' interest in contacting the lost respondents. This is a common procedure in some Latin American countries for contacting individuals and, if a convincing case is made, persons knowledgeable of the respondents' current address may provide researchers with the information.

Researchers interested in utilizing any of the suggestions mentioned above should keep in mind that they will often find Hispanics resistant to provide personal information about themselves or their friends to strangers. Most of this resistance is based on negative experiences with government and law enforcement agencies. For this reason, a researcher should quickly establish legitimacy during the initial contact through identification cards, official letters, sponsorship of respected community leaders, or support by church officials. Also, researchers should carefully find ways to safeguard the respondents' privacy and to demonstrate the safeguarding of that privacy. When necessary, the researcher can avoid directly requesting the address and telephone number of the respondent but rather ask the newly found informant, who knows of the whereabouts of the respondent, to address and mail a letter inviting the respondent to contact the researchers. In this case, the envelope should be open and with postage already paid when given to the informant.

Panel maintenance is certainly a difficult task for most researchers, and the sociodemographic characteristics of many Hispanics—including the high mobility rates common among the recently migrated—make it difficult to recontact Hispanics some time after the initial interview. The strategies to be implemented depend on the requirements of the actual study and the financial capabilities of the researchers. Here are some basic suggestions for panel maintenance:

Researchers needing to contact participants more than once should implement a careful panel maintenance strategy that at a minimum should include (a) obtaining the names and addresses of at least two relatives or friends of the respondent together with their place of employment; and, (b) maintaining periodic contact through the use of greeting cards, newsletters, and other correspondence (e.g., requesting address correction from the Postal Service).

Efforts should be made to find respondents lost to follow-up that include at a minimum searching telephone directories and through directory assistance and contacting neighbors, former employers, and other relevant institutions (churches, schools, consulates).

In implementing any of the suggested strategies for locating lost respondents, care should be given to demonstrate clearly the project's legitimacy in order to calm informants' fears regarding the use of the information.

This chapter has presented a series of alternatives available to researchers for contacting Hispanic participants and for obtaining accurate and relevant data or information. The following chapters deal with the procedures needed for the development of culturally appropriate instruments and for the analysis of data obtained from the respondents.

4

Development and Adaptation
of Instruments

In most social science research, human behavior is "measured" in some manner, whether it be through observational or rating protocols, attitude scales, personality or psychological tests, questionnaires, interview schedules, or projective stimuli. Since research is a human, not entirely objective process, these measures reflect the culturally based world view of those individuals doing the research, including their perceptions, norms, values, and biases. This chapter summarizes reasons for conducting research with culturally sensitive and culturally appropriate instruments and presents specific suggestions for creating or adapting instruments in order to reflect properly the culture of those included in the study.

A central concern of researchers involved with minority communities or, for that matter, engaging in cross-cultural research is ensuring the cultural appropriateness of the instrument to be used in the research project. In its simplest form, the underlying question is whether the research stimuli are being presented in equivalent ways to all of the individuals included in a study. The answer to this question lies far beyond obtaining an appropriate translation for a given instrument (a topic covered in Chapter 5). It refers to the instrument's ability to reflect the cultural assumptions of the respondents' groups and not just those of the researchers' culture. As Berry (1969) suggested, the goal is to obtain instruments that will elicit responses that convey similar meanings to the members of the various groups (i.e., "conceptual equivalence").

Given its significance, it is important to reiterate here that the development of culturally appropriate instruments, as well as of culturally appropriate procedures, research protocols, and interventions implies going beyond a simple translation or adaptation. In this sense, it is not enough to obtain a good translation of an instrument. It is also insufficient to ask members of an ethnic group to review and edit an instrument that was previously available to make it more appropriate or acceptable to the respondents. Likewise, changing examples or contexts in which questions are framed is not enough to produce a culturally appropriate instrument. As argued below, the development of a culturally appropriate measurement requires conducting basic developmental research that properly identifies the group-specific values, norms and expectations—the whole weltanschauung—of a group.

An example of what we suggest as inappropriate instrument development may clarify this further. Let's assume that a group of well-meaning researchers wish to measure the attitudes of Hispanic adolescents toward the consumption of alcoholic beverages. These researchers have previously used a scale they developed with non-Hispanic Whites to measure the use of alcoholic beverages and that scale has shown good reliability and validity. In their study with Hispanics they follow one of the better methods for translation (outlined in Chapter 5) and now have a Spanish version of their instrument. In addition, they call in a group of Hispanics residing in the area where they are going to conduct the study and ask them to indicate aspects of the questionnaire that should be changed in order to make it more appropriate for Hispanics. The group of consultants suggests changing the names of people to Hispanic names (e.g., changing John to Juan), changing the cultural content of the questions to reflect Hispanic events (mentioning the Cinco de Mayo holiday rather than the Fourth of July), changing the setting (including the questions within the context of a barrio), and using Spanish slang words for drinking and becoming intoxicated.

While these changes may be necessary and commendable, the researchers have not gone far enough. The researchers' assumption that the constructs to be studied have cultural universality is incorrect. By deciding to translate their instrument rather than develop a new one that reflects the culture of their respondents, they run the serious risk of missing key cultural aspects of the respondents' behavior. These researchers have failed to consider the group-specific world views of Hispanics in developing their instrument and have imposed the perceptions of non-Hispanics in the translated version. The next section of this chapter further exemplifies the problems that can arise when instruments are not culturally appropriate.

THE NEED FOR
CULTURALLY APPROPRIATE INSTRUMENTS

Individuals unfamiliar with cross-cultural research often have difficulty understanding the need to achieve cultural equivalence in instrumentation. This need may be better understood when recalling the difficulties experienced at one time or another while communicating with individuals who do not speak our language. Often the expressions are stilted or quaint, and the message becomes so confusing that its meaning is lost. For example, consider the experiences of a recently arrived Mexican colleague who answered his first telephone call in the United States by saying "Good?"—a literal translation of "¿Bueno?," the customary greeting in Mexico when answering telephone calls. These experiences help us realize that translations and adaptations must properly reflect not only our reality but that of all individuals who will participate in a given study.

The confusions and misinterpretations common when individuals from different cultures try to communicate with each other are the results of assessing reality from one personal perspective without considering that other cultural groups may perceive the same phenomenon differently. Consider a baseball fan who is watching a softball game but assumes the rules are the same as in baseball. The two games are similar in most details (shape of playing field, equipment, basic rules) but differ on such details as the number of players (four outfielders in softball instead of three in baseball) and the criteria for strikeouts (third foul for softball). A baseball fan who has never seen softball before would be confused to see "too many" players (10 instead of 9) and to find that playing rules are being "ignored."

As mentioned above, when conducting research with ethnic groups or across cultures researchers need to go beyond the proper translation of their original questions or topics into the other language. The issues or constructs studied must be meaningful to each of the research participants in the various cultures or groups and questions must be phrased in a way that will allow the researchers to measure equivalent constructs in all groups. While the emphasis in this chapter is on the development of culturally appropriate instruments, cultural appropriateness should be considered in all aspects of research: when planning a study, during the development of the instruments, when analyzing the data, and as the results are interpreted (Rogler, 1989).

A good example of the importance of assessing the culturally appropriate constructs is recounted by Lloyd Rogler (1989) in his study of families of schizophrenics in San Juan, Puerto Rico. One of the constructs to be studied was family decision making, a topic easily measured among non-Hispanic Whites by asking respondents to indicate who makes decisions such as where to go on a vacation, which schools the children should attend, or types of insurance to be bought. Initial contacts with the targeted respondents (slum residents of San Juan) indicated that these questions were irrelevant to the respondents since their financial situation never allowed or required those types of decisions. An alternative explored by the researchers was to change the wording of the items, but further pretesting and contact with the respondents showed that the concept of marital decision making was inappropriate since decision making implies choice, and individuals at that level of impoverishment do not have choices even in terms of basic personal needs such as types of food and clothing. The concept of decision making was discarded and replaced with that of division of labor. The latter concept was appropriate and relevant to the circumstances of the group to be studied and allowed the researchers to analyze the family dynamics of schizophrenic individuals (Rogler & Hollingshead, 1985).

UNIVERSAL VERSUS
GROUP-SPECIFIC CONCEPTS

Cross-cultural researchers have long been aware of the importance of assessing culturally appropriate constructs. One of the most important contributions of cross-cultural psychologists to research methodology in the social and behavioral sciences has been the distinction between what is universal (or "etic") and what is group-specific (or "emic"). The labels "etic" and "emic" may not seem very descriptive, but they represent a good simile, derived as they are from the suffixes utilized in linguistics to differentiate phonemics (language-specific sounds) from phonetics (universal sounds).

An example (Brislin, 1980) of the distinction between what is etic and what is emic is found in research on the need for achievement among Pacific Islanders (Gallimore, Weiss, & Finney, 1974). When studied in the United States, achievement motivation has been found to be independent from the need for affiliation. As such it is easy to find people engaged in achievement-oriented activities independent of their level of liking for their coworkers. Among Hawaiians, the two constructs have been found to interact so that achievement was important when it was related to the promotion of affiliation (e.g., giving money away). While the need for achievement seems to be universal, the relationship or independence of the construct is culture-specific, being independent of affiliation in the continental United States but closely related to affiliation among Hawaiians.

Another example of the distinction between universal and group-specific constructs is found in social scripts, or expected behavioral patterns for social situations (Triandis, Marín, Lisansky & Betancourt, 1984). As mentioned in Chapter 1, *simpatía* is a cultural script specific to Hispanics. Other scripts include *philotimo* (doing whatever ingroup members expect) among the Greeks (Feldman, 1968; Triandis, 1972) and *amae* (passive dependence) among the Japanese (Doi, 1973). The fact that different social scripts exist in various countries around the world allows us to think of social scripts in general as etic (universal) constructs while specific manifestations (i.e., *simpatía, philotimo, amae*) are demonstrations of the emic (group-specific) variations of the construct.

A danger in cross-cultural research is to assume erroneously the universality of a concept or construct. Whenever universality is assumed, it is called an *imposed etic* (Berry, 1969) or *pseudoetic* (Triandis, 1972). These are cases where the researcher imposes a world view that is culture-specific by assuming that those constructs or ideas are universally held. This assumption of universality is different from cases in which the universality (or panculturality) of etic constructs has been empirically demonstrated. Constructs shown through research data to be universal are called *derived etic* (Berry, 1969) to differentiate them from the other two. For example, translating an intelligence test into Spanish and applying it to Spanish-speaking Hispanics is an example of improperly assuming universality (pseudoetics). A process of derived etics would imply at the very least, the analysis of the items included in the test to make sure that they are culturally relevant. At the same time, the proper interpretation of the results would require carrying out new construct validation procedures as well as the identification of updated psychometric indices such as reliability coefficients and group norms.

Cross-cultural researchers have often argued that pseudoetic constructs or instruments should be avoided (e.g., Triandis, Malpass, & Davidson, 1973). Instead, researchers should create instruments that more properly reflect the cultural assumptions of the respondents. In fact, including items or constructs that are etic (universal) as well as emic (group-specific) in a research instrument can be expected to produce a clearer picture of the characteristics of a given group. In a test of this assumption, Triandis and Marín (1983) found that more culture-specific characteristics were found when Hispanics and non-Hispanic Whites were asked to respond to an instrument that included emic and etic items than when a pseudoetic instrument measuring the same topics (expected role-specific behaviors) was administered to a similar sample of respondents. The use of culturally appropriate instruments showed a complete and probably more accurate image of the psychological reality being studied in that research project.

DEVELOPING CULTURALLY APPROPRIATE INSTRUMENTS

A number of suggestions have been made by researchers concerning the development of culturally appropriate instruments. Three of the most useful suggestions (cultural immersion, consultation with experts or key informants, and Triandis's subjective culture approach) are reviewed below.

Cultural Immersion of Researchers

Many individuals (e.g., Marsella, 1978; Rogler, 1989) have argued that researchers should become immersed in the culture of the ethnic group they are going to study. This suggestion is based on the experiences of many anthropologists and other social scientists who would argue that a culture can best be understood from within itself. Among ethnic groups in the United States, immersion means more than just visiting ethnic areas of a city, eating at ethnic restaurants, shopping in that community, or being exposed to the ethnic media, although immersion may include all of these. Immersion in a culture implies experiencing and living in a culture in the same way that "natives" do. Ideally, researchers start perceiving reality in a way that resembles the outlook of the members of the group they are studying. Although it is difficult to specify the steps or procedures that researchers must follow in order to become immersed in a culture, the process certainly includes coming into contact with members of the cultural group in the most common human activities (eating, shopping, working, etc.) as well as studying the cultural products of the group (media, literature, plastic arts, music). Becoming immersed in a cultural group is certainly a difficult task that requires time and the particular ability to be a good observer and student of human behavior.

As could be expected, the approaches developed by anthropologists, sociologists, and ecological psychologists (e.g., Fetterman, 1989; Jorgensen, 1989) are particularly useful here as these allow the researcher to observe and interact with the culture and to become part of it from the beginning of the study. The major drawback of some participatory approaches to observation is the subjective interpretation of reality on the part of the researchers. In these cases, *validity checks* can be instituted by contrasting the observations of researchers becoming immersed in a group with those of other individuals who are better acquainted with the specific ethnic group. Researchers interested in studying Hispanics, for example, can become immersed in the culture by interacting with Hispanics in their ethnic communities (e.g., Hialeah in Dade County, Florida, the Bronx in New York, the Mission District in San Francisco, or East Los Angeles) and then checking their observations with Hispanic social scientists or other researchers who may have been in the field longer.

Becoming familiar with a culture allows the researcher to interact with the physical (e.g., literature, arts, architecture) and subjective (e.g., values, attitudes) aspects of a culture from the same perspectives utilized by individuals who were raised in the culture. In sum, becoming immersed in a culture allows researchers to perceive reality in a manner similar to that of the members of the culture.

Contact with Key Informants

In some cases, of course, physical immersion in a culture is not possible due to time limitations, financial constraints, or other reasons. Another approach to identifying cultural differences is the use of key informants (Brislin, 1986; Wesley & Karr, 1966). Key informants are individuals or researchers who are knowledgeable about the culture in question and who can sensitize the investigator to the culture-specific aspects of the study and provide information on how to make the procedures culturally appropriate.

Investigators planning to conduct research with a cultural, ethnic, or racial group that is new to them should consult the anthropological studies reported in research monographs or books. Also useful are the various ethnographies referenced in the Human Relations Area Files (HRAF). These are available at many university libraries and deal primarily with less industrialized cultural groups (for a description of these files see Barry, 1980).

A large number of books and articles have been written about Hispanic culture as a whole as well as about the primary Hispanic subgroups. In a review of the literature conducted in 1981, Judith Lisansky was able to identify over 200 significant publications dealing with aspects of Hispanic culture from the perspective of the social or behavioral sciences. Below is a list of major works on Hispanics that can serve as a point of departure for researchers new to the field. Readers should note that a number of publications have been excluded from this listing. The list is meant as a starting point. A few early, seminal books have been included because of their length and comprehensiveness, but researchers also should utilize recent journal articles that can be accessed through the usual citation and bibliographic search mechanisms. One especially noteworthy source is the *Hispanic Journal of Behavioral Sciences,* which has been published quarterly for over then years and is now printed and distributed by Sage Publications. The early citations to Hispanic research are found in Newton, Olmedo, and Padilla (1982).

Mexican-Americans

Achor, S. C. (1978). *Mexican Americans in a Dallas barrio.* Tucson: University of Arizona Press.

Burma, J. H. (1970). *Mexican Americans in the United States: A reader.* Cambridge, MA: Schenkman.

Gonzalez, N. L. (1969). *The Spanish-Americans of New Mexico.* Albuquerque: University of New Mexico Press.

Grebler, L., Moore, J. W., & Guzman, R. C. (1970). *The Mexican-American people: The nation's second largest minority.* New York: Free Press.

Heller, C. S. (1966). *Mexican-American youth: Forgotten youth at the crossroads.* New York: Random House.

Hernandez, C. A., Haug, M. J., & Wagner, N. N. (1976). *Chicanos: Social and psychological perspectives.* St. Louis: Mosby.

Martinez, J. L., & Mendoza, R. H. (1984). *Chicano psychology.* New York: Academic Press.

Moore, J. W. (1976). *Mexican Americans.* New York: Prentice-Hall.

Cuban-Americans

Fagen, R. R., Brody, R. A. & O'Leary, T. J. (1968). *Cubans in exile.* Stanford, CA: Stanford University Press.

Rogg, E. (1974). *The assimilation of Cuban exiles.* New York: Aberdeen.

Rogg, E. M., & Santana Cooney, R. (1980). *Adaptation and adjustment of Cubans: West New York, New Jersey.* New York: Hispanic Research Center, Fordham University.

Puerto Ricans

Fitzpatrick, J. P. (1987). *Puerto Rican Americans.* Englewood Cliffs, NJ: Prentice-Hall.

Padilla, E. (1964). *Up from Puerto Rico.* New York: Columbia University Press.
Rogler, L. H. (1972). *Migrants in the city: The life of a Puerto Rican action group.* New York: Basic Books.
Wagenheim, K. (1975). *A survey of Puerto Ricans on the U.S. mainland in the 1970s.* New York: Praeger.

To summarize, basic to the development of culturally appropriate instruments and research protocols is the development of a significant level of familiarity with the culture's basic characteristics. This implies the following:

> When planning studies with members of an unfamiliar ethnic or cultural group, researchers should immerse themselves in all aspects of the culture so that they are able to perceive the world from the perspective of the individuals being studied.
>
> To gain knowledge about a new ethnic group, the researcher should contact social scientists or key informants who can provide validity checks on the researcher's observations.
>
> Researchers need to become familiar with basic writings in the social sciences concerning the group being studied. Current research in the social and behavioral sciences as well as classics in the field should be consulted.

The Analysis of a Group's Subjective Culture

Harry Triandis (1972) has suggested a strategy for developing culturally appropriate instruments that is based on a large number of studies conducted in cultures as varied as India, Japan, Greece, Latin America, and the United States. The premise of this strategy of instrument development is that researchers need to become aware of the etic (universal) and emic (culture-specific) aspects of the constructs or behaviors to be measured in order to reflect properly the reality being studied. Comparisons across cultural groups can then be made utilizing elements of reality perceived by both researchers and respondents.

The analysis of the subjective culture of a group is defined by Triandis (1972) as the process by which consistencies or patterns in responses by members of a group are extracted and then drawn on a map that identifies the group's cognitive structure. The term *subjective culture* is used to refer to the nonphysical aspects of a culture (as opposed to objective culture, which refers to physical aspects such as pottery, housing, literature, art). It is assumed that these consistencies in responses are mediated by constructs such as attitudes, norms, values, and expectancies that are specific to a given class of social stimuli. The consistencies in these constructs, posited to be the products of a shared culture and of propinquity, enhance the chances for frequent interaction among the members of the group. In addition, race, gender, age, or sexual preferences also can be perceived as furthering the chances of ingroup interaction and of the development of a unique subjective culture for individuals who share certain sociodemographic character-istics (e.g., older Black males).

Triandis (1972) has suggested that a study of the subjective culture of a group should include certain psychological constructs that are pan-cultural and that help develop the map of the group's understanding of social reality. Among those constructs one finds cognitive associations, attitudes, beliefs, categorizations, evaluations, expectations, memories, opinions, role perceptions, stereotypes, and values. The measurement of all of these various constructs is time-consuming, so researchers will probably want to choose those that are most appropriate to their goals. On the one hand, if the object of a study is to identify as complete a cognitive map of the group as possible, then probably all of the constructs should be studied. If, on the other hand, the interest of the researcher is to identify some specific characteristics, then a subset of the constructs may be sufficient. For example, in some of our studies on the subjective culture of cigarette smoking, we found that the ex-pectations about the consequences of the behavior were more useful in developing health-promotion messages (Marín, Marín, Pérez-Stable, Otero-Sabogal, & Sabogal, 1990) than some of the other components suggested by Triandis (e.g., stereotypes of smokers). This strategy for the creation of culturally appropriate instruments has been used widely in basic sociopsychological research to identify Hispanic culture-specific values and norms as well as in applied settings such as on the promotion of smoking cessation (Marín, Marín, Otero-Sabogal, Sabogal, & Pérez-Stable, 1989). Given its usefulness, we will describe in detail Triandis's methodology.

The research strategy for conducting subjective culture studies incor-porates methods used by most social scientists including surveying respondents with open- and closed-ended questions. The development of materials to study the subjective culture of a group involves two steps. In step one, themes, issues, and associations that are salient among the group's members are elicited through open-ended questions. In step two, a map of the subjective culture is created by identifying the differences and similarities in the perceptions of the constructs being studied that are present in a group, between two groups, or among more than two groups. The second step involves closed-ended questionnaires developed after the results of step one have been content analyzed. The process is described in greater detail below.

Step one. In step one of a subjective culture analysis, verbal responses to a set of topics are elicited from a number of individuals. The topics are chosen by the researchers because of their importance for an understanding of the issue being studied. The end result of this step is the identification of stems and response categories that are culturally appropriate to the ethnic or cultural group being studied.

In carrying out step one, the researchers need to generate open-ended questions that target the sociopsychological construct or the behavior of interest and that will generate a variety of responses on the part of the research participants. For example, in studying adolescent cigarette smoking the researcher could individually interview a number of adolescents with questions such as "What takes place right before you try a cigarette?" or "How do you feel right before you smoke?" These questions would measure the perceived circumstances (antecedents) surrounding the behaviors of trying or smoking a cigarette. Attitudes could be studied by asking respondents a question such as "What negative consequences does smoking have for you?" while stereotypes could be studied by asking "What are smokers like?" or "What are boys who don't smoke like?"

Open-ended questions such as those mentioned above will produce a very rich sample of perceptions of a given behavior (such as cigarette smoking) or of their world views (e.g., parent-child relationships, job satisfaction). These responses are then content analyzed in order to identify the most representative or the most common responses by members of a given ethnic or cultural group. If the researchers were interested in studying Hispanics and non-Hispanic Whites, for example, they would look for three types of responses: (a) Hispanic emics, those responses frequent among Hispanics but absent or very infrequent among non-Hispanic Whites; (b) non-Hispanic White emics, those responses frequent among non-Hispanics but absent or very infrequent among Hispanics; and (c) etic responses, those answers common to both groups. As can be expected, some answers will be worded differently although the meaning is the same or fairly similar. For example, in reporting expected outcomes for quitting smoking, we obtained responses such as "I'll get fat" together with "I'll gain weight." In the content analysis, both of these responses were perceived to form part of the same expected consequence of quitting cigarette smoking.

Step two. Once the content analysis has been completed, the researcher will use responses from step one to generate the stems and/or response categories of the closed-ended questionnaires. The purpose of this second step is to obtain numerical responses to the issues identified during step one in order to identify more appropriately the culture-specific attitudes, values, norms, and expectancies of the ethnic or cultural groups being studied.

The question format for step two will now include a specific stem related to the subjective culture construct in question (e.g., antecedents of cigarette smoking by adolescents) together with a number of possible events or behaviors. For example, in the case of a study on adolescent cigarette smoking, the antecedents could be studied by a stem such as "How likely is it that if A1. . . A10, then you will try a cigarette?" In this case, A1 through A10 would be the antecedents identified as part of step one (e.g., "someone offers you a cigarette," "you hang out with the guys," "you are at a party"). These antecedents would have been identified through the content analysis carried out in step one and represent etic (universal) ideas as well as Hispanic *and* non-Hispanic emic (group-specific) responses. One possible item then would read, "How likely is it that if you are at a party, you will try a cigarette?" while another item would read, "How likely is it that if you hang out with the guys, then you will try a cigarette?"

The actual number of items generated in this part of the process will depend on the number of responses elicited during Step One. In the example we have considered 10 possible antecedents: A1 through A10, where A1 could be "are at a party" and A2 may be "hang out with the guys." Once the closed-ended items are generated, respondents can be asked to answer on a Likert-type scale or by using some other numerical scale. These scales may measure likelihood of the event (e.g., 1 = Very Unlikely; 5 = Very Likely), evaluation of the statement (e.g., 1 = Very Bad; 5 = Very Good) or level of agreement with the phrase (1 = Disagree; 5 = Agree).

The data obtained from the closed-ended questionnaires in step two can be analyzed using a number of procedures. When more than one ethnic group is studied, factor analyses with multiple rotations should be conducted separately for items related to each important construct and separately for each ethnic group. For example, one factor analysis would be conducted for antecedents of smoking among Hispanic respondents and a second for antecedents of smoking for non-Hispanic Whites. These factor analyses will identify similarities and differences between ethnic groups in the way in which they perceive a given construct. It can be argued that items have equivalent meaning across ethnic groups when the factor analyses of the data from the two ethnic groups show similar item loadings on the same factors. When this is true, these items can be subjected to multivariate and univariate inferential analyses in order to identify culture-specific differences across groups.

The above procedures have been successfully utilized recently to identify basic aspects of Hispanic culture (e.g., Triandis et al., 1982; Triandis, Marín, Hui, Lisansky & Ottati, 1984; Triandis, Marín, Lisansky & Betancourt, 1984) as well as the culture-specific components of a culturally appropriate community health promotion campaign (Marín, Marín, Otero-Sabogal, Sabogal, & Pérez-Stable, 1990; Marín, Pérez-Stable, Otero-Sabogal, Sabogal & Marín, 1989). In a study identifying basic Hispanic role perceptions (Triandis, Marín, Hui, Lisansky, & Ottati, 1984), Hispanic respondents were found to have a strong pull toward the family and to show some ambivalence toward the job environment. Non-Hispanic Whites on the other hand, showed a movement away from the family and a pull toward work, with the total sum of the forces favoring work roles over family roles.

On the applied side, our research using Triandis's suggestions for the study of subjective culture with cigarette smokers has shown that Hispanics differ from non-Hispanic White smokers in a number of sociopsychological characteristics: Hispanics are more likely to perceive smokers as nervous, friendly, sociable, and aggressive; smoking is perceived by Hispanics as a social behavior and as less dependent on situational and emotional cues than it is for non-Hispanics. Our research using Triandis's suggestions has also shown that Hispanics are very concerned about the short-term effects of smoking (bad breath, criticisms from the family) and the bad example smoking gives to their children (Marín, Marín, Pérez-Stable, Otero-Sabogal, & Sabogal, 1990). Based on these data, a culturally appropriate community intervention was developed that has proven effective in changing perceptions and levels of information of the individuals targeted (Marín, Marín, Pérez-Stable, Sabogal, & Otero-Sabogal, 1990).

In summary, the subjective culture analysis of a group can be carried out to identify culture-specific and culture-universal aspects of a group's world view. This process will help the researcher produce culturally appropriate instruments and research protocols that will enhance the quality of the data and their heuristic value.

A subjective culture study is an effective way of identifying etic (group-specific) and emic (universal) aspects of a group's values, attitudes, norms, expectancies, stereotypes, beliefs, and roles.

To carry out a subjective culture study of a group, researchers should first elicit from a small number of individuals a large set of response categories associated with each of the constructs to be studied. A content analysis of these responses will provide the response categories for closed-ended questions.

As the second step, the closed-ended questions should be applied to a larger number of respondents and analyzed using factor analysis as well as multivariate and univariate statistics.

ISSUES WITH THE USE OF STANDARDIZED INSTRUMENTS

In many cases, researchers in the social and behavioral sciences prefer to use standardized or previously developed instruments to measure personality or psychopathology (e.g., psychological or psychiatric scales, personality tests) or social behaviors (e.g., social support, attitude scales, opinion surveys). Unfortunately, such instruments are commonly used by researchers without considering differences in the psychometric characteristics of their instruments when used with a culturally different group of respondents.

Various studies have shown that the internal structure of an instrument changes when it is adapted and translated into Spanish. Garza (1977) for example, has found that the well-known scale for the measurement of internal-external locus of control developed by Rotter produced different factor structures when applied to Mexican-Americans than those found among non-Hispanic Whites. Thus, Rotter's scale measures two different constructs when applied to Hispanics and non-Hispanic Whites. Different factor structures also have been found for various well-known psychological instruments when translated and adapted for use in Latin America. The Minnesota Multiphasic Personality Inventory (MMPI), for example, has shown different factor structures when used in translation in Argentina (De Barbenza & Montoya, 1979), Cuba (Gonzalez Valdes, 1979), and the United States among Hispanics (Reschly, 1978) from those originally reported for the English version of the test. These differences in factor structures also have been found for translations of Rokeach's Value Scale (Gunther, 1981);

Eysenck's Personality Inventory (Garcia Sevilla, Pérez, & Tobena, 1979); for a well-known measure of depression, the Center for Epidemiological Studies Depression Scale (CES-D; Guarnaccia, Angel, & Worobey, 1989); and for other tests (Nelson, Knight, Kagan, & Gumbiner, 1980).

Other psychometric characteristics also may change when instruments are translated into Spanish and utilized with Hispanics or Latin Americans. Henggeler and Tavormina (1979) have shown that translations of such widely used tests as the Weschler Intelligence Scale and the Peabody Picture Vocabulary Test have poorer reliability scores in Spanish than in their original versions. The Diagnostic Interview Schedule (DIS) has shown different distribution of results when applied in Puerto Rico and in the United States, forcing the researchers to choose cutoff scores for Puerto Rico that are different from those utilized in the United States (Bird, Canino, & Shrout, 1985). A recent study has further shown that instruments lose certain important psychometric characteristics when translated and adapted (Deyo, 1984). The Sickness Impact Profile (SIP) was applied to Mexican-Americans in Texas either in English or in Spanish and their scores compared with various clinical measures of disease severity in order to measure the construct validity of the SIP. The data showed that while the internal consistency of both versions was high, the scores for the SIP were valid in English but not in Spanish.

Once an instrument has been translated following the suggestions presented in Chapter 5, researchers must make sure that the Spanish version of the instrument is fully equivalent to the English-language version (Flaherty, 1987). First, researchers should analyze the internal structure of the instrument as well as its internal consistency. Procedures such as factor analysis can provide a good indication of the factor structures inherent in the item responses of Hispanics as compared to non-Hispanic Whites. A measurement of the internal consistency of the instrument (e.g., coefficient alpha) also should be obtained.

In addition, researchers need to identify other psychometric characteristics of the instruments to be used in a research project. Of particular importance is a measure of the validity of the instrument in order to make sure that the instrument continues to measure what it purports to measure. Finally, an indication of the distributions of the scores in the population and psychometric norms of the test should be obtained. Based on these results, the researchers can establish cutoff scores for the identification of groups (e.g., depressed vs. not depressed individuals) and to compare their respondents with those of other studies.

Procedures for obtaining these psychometric measures are described in standard psychometric texts and should be consulted by researchers planning to use any type of standardized instrument. Unfortunately, very few currently available standardized tests have undergone a thorough psychometric analysis of their Spanish versions (Malgady, Rogler, & Constantino, 1987).

The procedures described above that must be followed before using a standardized test or scale are expensive and time-consuming. In many cases it is better to develop a new instrument that more adequately reflects the characteristics of the groups to be studied. The subjective culture procedure described above is optimal in this regard.

The researcher must consider the potential lack of comparability across ethnic or cultural groups before translating a paper-and-pencil instrument.

> Whenever a researcher utilizes a paper-and-pencil measurement instrument not previously standardized for Hispanics, efforts should be made to obtain at least the following measures:
>
> (1) an indication of the internal structure of the instrument (factor analysis of the responses can provide information regarding this important characteristic of an instrument);
> (2) a measurement of the reliability of the instrument (e.g., alpha coefficient);
> (3) tests of the instrument's validity; and
> (4) a description of the distribution of the instrument's scores (e.g., mean, mode, median, standard deviation, kurtosis).

In this chapter we have argued for the need to develop instruments that reflect the cultural characteristics of the respondents. It is hoped that future researchers will pay the same attention to the development of culturally appropriate instruments as they do to other aspects of the research process. Data obtained with poorly developed instruments are uninterpretable due to the plausible rival hypothesis of differential instrumentation.

5

Translation of Data Collection Instruments

As previously mentioned in this book, a significant proportion of adult Hispanics in the United States do not speak English (approximately 25%) and a larger proportion (65%) prefer to use Spanish in their normal day-to-day interactions. These figures imply that researchers interested in studying Hispanics will need to have their data collection instruments available in both English and Spanish. Investigators need to consider the translation of their instruments as one of the most important steps in their research project, equivalent in significance to the original process of instrument development or even data collection and interpretation. An improper translation may make it impossible to answer the questions for which the study was originally designed.

In any study with members of ethnic or cultural groups that utilize different languages, researchers must be sure that the plausible rival hypothesis of differential instrumentation has been ruled out (Brislin, 1970). This consideration forces the researcher to make sure that when studying a group such as Hispanics in the United States, the Spanish version of the instruments is equivalent to the English version. If the translation process does not produce two fully equivalent versions of the data collection instruments, differences found between the respondents may be due to the fact that they responded to two different instruments, one in English that measured constructs that may differ from those studied with the Spanish version (Brown & Sechrest, 1980).

A central concern of every translation is to produce the *cultural equivalent* of an instrument (Werner & Campbell, 1970). A culturally equivalent version of the original instrument is one that has equivalent connotative meaning. In this sense, the translation process needs to go beyond finding the equivalent denotative meaning of the words used in the original version (literal translation) in order to capture the connotations or implied associations of the words. The identification of this connotative meaning is a process that surpasses finding the words' explicit (denotative) meaning in order to reflect properly their implied meaning as used by the researchers when drafting the instruments.

82

There is ample evidence that differences exist in the connotation of certain words in English and in Spanish. Diaz-Guerrero and Peck (1963), for example, have found that the Spanish equivalent for the word "respect" has overtones of obedience, duty, and deference in Mexico while in the United States "respect" signifies admiration and subordination. These findings suggest that the English word "respect" may not have the same meaning as its Spanish denotative equivalent ("*respeto*")and that researchers using this word need to understand its connotation in the language of the original instrument before using it in a different language.

Another example of the need to understand properly the different meanings of a word can be seen in a study conducted in Uganda to explore familial lineage (Adams, 1974). In questions dealing with the enumeration of relatives, respondents were asked to list separately all of their siblings and, later, all of their cousins. The translators failed to recognize the fact that traditional versions of the Luganda language do not have separate words for cousins and siblings and utilized the same word in both questions. The data showed that a large number of respondents listed all of their siblings and all of their cousins in both questions. The translators' inability to recognize the implied meanings of the words being used rendered those questions useless to the researcher.

It should be noted that translation is of concern not only to the data-oriented scientist who utilizes questionnaires, interview schedules, behavioral observation checklists, and similar instruments but also to those researchers interested in qualitative research. Various authors (e.g., Sechrest, Fay, & Zaidi, 1972) have argued that investigators conducting qualitative research with individuals from linguistic groups different from their own need to consider the translation of various research components. Among these are the study's objective as presented to the participants or consultants; the instructions given to the participants; the specific research tools; and the consultants' responses or remarks.

This chapter summarizes the procedures that researchers can follow in order to produce culturally equivalent English and Spanish forms of their interview schedule, observation forms, questionnaires, or any other research or data collection instrument. Suggestions also are made for ways in which researchers can check the appropriateness of the translation of the instruments they plan to utilize.

THE VARIABILITY OF WRITTEN
AND SPOKEN SPANISH

A note of caution is required at the outset regarding the variability of spoken and written Spanish in Latin America and in the United States. Contemporary Spanish as used by the majority of Latin Americans and United States Hispanics is a stable, universally understood language. This standard Spanish goes beyond national and regional frontiers and backgrounds and is utilized in the United States by television and radio networks such as Univision and Telemundo. Thus, radio and television announcers and news commentators use a Spanish that is understood by all Spanish speakers in the United States (broadcasting Spanish) that uses basic vocabulary, grammar, and syntax. In addition, this broadcasting Spanish utilizes a standard (nonregional) accent and lilt. This is equivalent to the broadcasting English that is utilized by television networks in the United States that not only avoids regional accents (e.g., New Yorker, Southerner) but also avoids a vocabulary that is regionalized or limited in acceptance (e.g., avoids using "bubbler" for water fountain or "pop" for soft drink).

There is, therefore, a Spanish language that is understood and utilized by most individuals who consider themselves to be Spanish-speakers irrespective of the part of the country in which they live or of the national origin of their families. This Spanish is basically the same language that is used in Spain or in Latin America and that allows a Puerto Rican residing in New York to speak to and be understood by a Cuban-American in Miami, a Mexican-American in San Antonio, or a Salvadoran in San Francisco.

Regional Variations

As with any vital language, there are vocabulary variations in Spanish that are based on nation-specific usage, a phenomenon that also occurs with other modern languages that are spoken by a variety of peoples. English-speakers in the United Kingdom, for example, often utilize one word to name a particular referent while a different word is utilized in the United States for the same object (e.g., "lift" for elevator or "pram" for baby carriage). Vocabulary differences in Spanish across nations are usually found in the words that denote flowers, fruits, and certain vegetables as well as for sexual behaviors. In these cases, there may be country-specific names applied to a given object (for example "*china*" as used in Puerto Rico to denote the fruit of the orange tree) or vocabulary preferences that are more regional in nature. Recently, Fishman (1987) estimated that the rate of usage of these regional variations is diminishing in the Spanish printed media of the United States, reflecting what he considers is also occurring in spoken Spanish among Hispanics.

Researchers will need to be aware of regional variations that may be present in the vocabulary to be used as part of a study. Three possible solutions to the problem of regional variations in vocabulary are described below.

Use all appropriate variations of a word. For written instruments, whenever the respondents represent various subgroups, researchers should include all relevant vocabulary variations in the research protocols. For example, if Puerto Ricans are to be included in a sample of Hispanics and respondents need to think of oranges (e.g., in a nutrition survey where consumption of oranges is being measured), the researcher should utilize both commonly used words: "*¿Cuántas naranjas o chinas come usted en una semana?*"

Target vocabulary variations to each subgroup. For studies where the subgroup identification of the respondents as well as the group-specific vocabulary preferences are known, investigators should use group-specific vocabulary. In trying to measure the consumption of cigars by Hispanic respondents in the H-HANES, it was noted that the three Hispanic subgroups to be studied utilized different words to refer to a cigar. The question was phrased so that the interview schedule included the three common names used among Hispanics to refer to a cigar but only the subgroup-specific variant was used by the interviewer: "*¿Cuántos puros/tabacos/cigarros fuma por día mas o menos?*," with *cigarros* being used with Puerto Ricans, *tabacos* with Cubans, and *puros* with Mexican-Americans (Treviño, 1985).

Avoid colloquialisms. In some cases, the vocabulary preferred by one group may produce confusions when members of a different Hispanic subgroup are exposed to it. This is particularly true of colloquialisms but may also be a problem with other words. For example, a colloquial expression to denote a bus in Puerto Rico and in Cuba is *guagua* while this same word is used colloquially to denote a baby or a young child in Chile and a type of wolf in Colombia. A possible solution to this problem is of course to avoid colloquial expressions, which in any case may lend themselves to misinterpretations and confusion on the part of the research participants.

Use alternate phrases. In some cases the only solution to vocabulary confusions is alternate wording of the questions. The H-HANES found a problem with the word utilized to denote lunch in Spanish. While Puerto Ricans and Cubans use *"almuerzo"* to denote lunch, this same word is used by many Mexican Americans to refer to breakfast. In this case, the use of *"almuerzo"* would prove confusing to Mexican-Americans, so the researchers decided to use a descriptive sentence that would be conceptually equivalent for all of the respondents: *"la comida del mediodia,"* or the midday meal, instead of *"almuerzo"* (Treviño, 1985).

Variations Due to Mixing English and Spanish

Because Hispanics in the United States are surrounded by the English language, English words and grammar often seep into their daily language use. This mixing of English and Spanish can create problems for researchers. For example, bilingual Hispanics often mix English and Spanish words in the same sentence (e.g., *"Yo estaba leyendo cuando* it started to rain"). This code mixing is often found among Hispanics of second and higher generations who are more at ease expressing specific feelings or ideas in one of the two languages or who may have momentarily forgotten the appropriate word in the language they are using.

A second linguistic variation of importance is found among those individuals who anglicize certain words or who borrow English words to develop specific linguistic patterns (e.g., *"Está reinando"* for "It's raining," calling a grocery store a *"grocería,"* or using *"carpeta"* for rug instead of *"alfombra"*).

While these variations may be perplexing to a researcher unfamiliar with them, they can easily be handled by individuals who are sensitive to the linguistic characteristics of Hispanics in the United States. Researchers will need to be sensitive to these possible variations in language use and be ready to process properly any responses given in these mixed codes when doing participant observations or conducting open-ended interviews where the responses of the individuals being studied need to be recorded as given by the person being interviewed. In these cases it becomes imperative that the individuals carrying out the research be fluent not only in both languages (English and Spanish) but also in the linguistic variations that they might find. Needless to say, however, these variations should not be included in research protocols due to their limited acceptance and to the fact that they carry surplus meaning.

In groups where the spoken language includes English loans or calques (e.g., "*frizar*" for freezing or "*rufo*" for roof), or where grammatical and orthographic violations of Spanish norms are usual, researchers have found that instruments written in standard English and Spanish will usually be properly understood by individuals who ordinarily utilize these linguistic variations. Even those individuals who prefer nonstandard English or Spanish when speaking or writing can provide the researcher with appropriate responses using instruments in standard Spanish or English.

Researchers should include on their research team as staff or as consultants individuals who are familiar with the linguistic variations common among the population to be studied. This is particularly important when the respondents belong to groups that are counternormative (e.g., gangs, drug users) or who are isolated by others' prejudicial attitudes (e.g., actively homosexual men) and who may have developed a group-specific vocabulary. Carballo-Diéguez (1989) has recently discussed the difficulties involved in addressing Hispanic gays because the Spanish language does not have a neutral word equivalent to the word "gay" in English. He reports that Argentinian gays refer to other homosexuals as people who *entienden* (understand) while other Hispanic gays talk of each other as someone who is "in the action."

WRITING TRANSLATABLE ENGLISH

Due to its linguistic characteristics and the constant flux of its vocabulary, English is difficult to translate into Romance languages such as Spanish. Various researchers have made suggestions for writing translatable English that should be kept in mind when writing the original version of a data-gathering instrument in that language (e.g., Brislin, 1980; Brislin et al., 1973). These suggestions, detailed below, will make it easier for translators to produce a fully equivalent version of the original.

In order to produce translatable instruments, researchers should follow these guidelines:

> Use simple English (approximately third-grade-level English).
> Utilize when possible words that have Latin roots since those words are easier to translate into Romance languages (e.g., use "abundant" rather than "plentiful").

Use nouns rather than pronouns.

Avoid metaphors and colloquialisms. (It is difficult to translate expressions such as "right on," "feeling blue," or "awesome" and maintain the proper connotation.)

Avoid possessive forms that may be misinterpreted when more than one actor is involved (e.g., "his," "hers," "theirs").

Use specific rather than general terms (e.g., "ducks" rather than "fowl," "dogs" rather than "pets").

Avoid words that may indicate vagueness regarding some event (e.g., "probably," "frequently").

Use short and simple sentences of fewer than 16 words.

Utilize the active rather than the passive voice (e.g., "Samuel received the award" rather than "the award was received by Samuel").

Avoid the subjunctive (e.g., verb forms with could or would).

Avoid adverbs and prepositions telling where and when (e.g. "beyond," "often").

Avoid sentences with two different verbs if the verbs suggest different actions.

Use redundant wording to clarify the context and meaning of a phrase wherever possible.

TRANSLATION TECHNIQUES

There are three basic approaches to conducting a translation and each of them is known by labels that summarize the process: one-way translation, committee approach, and double translation. These three approaches are described below together with an examination of their limitations. Decentering is presented as an important adjunct to double translation.

One-Way Translation

Usually, a one-way translation implies asking a bilingual individual to translate the original version of a text or instrument into the target language. The translator will depend on his or her knowledge of both languages and the information that may be available in dictionaries and other reference materials in order to produce the version in the target language. Usually this translation procedure results in a version of the original that corresponds to the denotative rather than the connotative meaning of the original.

While this translation approach is appealing because of its simplicity and economy, it has significant limitations given that the work of one translator is left unchecked. The overreliance on one individual allows misinterpretations in meaning to become part of the instrument in the target language version. Misinterpretations by the translator can be produced by such factors as lack of language ability and fluidity, the presence of cultural concepts and behaviors that may be unfamiliar to the translator, as well as mistakes and inaccuracies present in the original version that were not caught by the researchers.

Further evidence for the limitations of the one-way translation approach is found in a recent study (Berkanovic, 1980) that showed that the Spanish version of an instrument translated in this fashion had lower reliability and lower bivariate correlation scores than its English version. This translation approach not only negatively affects the quality of the translation but also the psychometric characteristics of the instrument as a whole. *Given these reasons, the one-way translation approach should never be utilized.*

Translation by Committee

A second translation approach consists of asking two or more individuals who are familiar with both languages to translate separately the text or instrument from the original language into the target language. After the translation has been done, the investigator can either (a) ask the translators to meet, discuss their differences, and produce a final consensus version; or (b) ask an independent observer (e.g., a colleague or a language professor) to choose the version that seems most appropriate.

The committee approach has the advantage that it may be less time-consuming than double translation (discussed below) but it has some serious limitations. It is possible that the translators may share a common world view due to their education, social class, or linguistic experiences that may affect the accuracy of the translation. This is particularly true in those studies where researchers enlist the aid of their bilingual graduate students or colleagues in the foreign language department of a university to conduct the translation. A second limitation of this approach is the fact that committee discussions may be affected by cultural norms that proscribe disagreement with certain individuals (e.g., those with prestige, older persons, the more educated) or by the reluctance of individuals to criticize their colleagues. These social norms may produce the appearance of consensus among the members of the committee, concealing disagreements about the version being produced. The gains in time when using the translation by committee are undercut by the problems inherent in conducting such a translation.

Double Translation

This approach (also called "back translation") involves at least two bilingual individuals who participate independently in the translation process. In its simplest form, one translator takes the original version and translates it into the target language in much the same fashion as is done in the one-way translation approach described above. Once this target language version is ready, the second translator takes it and uses it to produce a new version of the instrument but this time in the language of the original version. For example, translator A (Juan) takes the English version of an interview schedule and translates it into Spanish. Once this is done, translator B (Rosa) takes the Spanish version produced by Juan and translates it into English. Each translator works independently and no consultation among them is allowed, although they are encouraged to use dictionaries and other reference works that may be useful in the process.

At the end of this phase of the translation, the researcher has two versions of the instrument in the original language and one version in the target language. Comparisons are then made of the two versions in the original language in order to identify inconsistencies between both versions. In the example above, the researcher would compare the original English version of the instrument produced by the research team and the version produced by Rosa from Juan's Spanish version. Inconsistencies between the English versions can include words that may have been mistranslated or sentences that lost or changed their meaning. Ideally, both versions in the original language should be identical. If differences are found, the researcher can consult with both translators in order to identify the reasons for the differences and to reach an agreement regarding the best alternative.

A better approach is to use more than one iteration and to engage more than two translators. In this case the instrument goes first from English to Spanish, then back to English. That second English version is then translated to Spanish and the second Spanish version is translated back to English. While this approach is more costly, it produces a better version of the instrument since it goes through a number of filters and versions that are produced independently by each of the translators.

There is evidence in the literature for the advantages of the double translation approach when obtaining Spanish-language versions of various types of instruments to be used with Hispanics in the United States. Lega (1981) and Santisteban and Szapocznik (1981), for example, have used it to translate a psychological assessment test, while we have used the approach extensively to translate survey questionnaires (Marín, Pérez-Stable, & Marín, 1989; Marín, Pérez-Stable, Otero-Sabogal, Sabogal, & Marín, 1989) and attitudinal scales (Marín, Sabogal, Marín, Otero-Sabogal, & Pérez-Stable, 1987). In all of these studies, the Spanish-language versions have proven to be equivalent to those originally produced in English.

The double translation approach, probably the most adequate translation procedure, can be summarized as follows:

The version in the original language is translated by translator A into the target language.

A second translator (translator B) takes the product of the previous step and independently translates it back into the original language.

The investigator compares both versions in the original language and checks with translators for inconsistencies.

A second round of translations may be necessary for sections in which there are a large number of inconsistencies.

While double translation is probably the best translation method available, it has some limitations that need to be taken into consideration. First, it is possible that the researcher may find identical versions in the original language that may have been produced not because the target language translation is appropriate but rather because the two translators share a common set of linguistic rules due to their common educational or socioeconomic background. These common world views may allow the translators to back-translate into the original language the idea initially expressed even if that idea is not properly represented in the target language version. This problem is more likely to occur when translators are bilingual but not bicultural and therefore can miss the nuances of a language.

Utilizing literal translations or using only the most common meaning of a word can cause misinterpretations of the connotative meaning of a word. For example, "friend" and its Spanish equivalent "*amigo*" can be used to mean, among other things, an acquaintance, a liked and trusted person, a supporter of a cause, a lover, and an ally. Which meaning is implied can be central to the translation of a sentence and in many cases this can only be ascertained by knowing the linguistic and cultural contexts. The English word "friend" may have been translated as "*amigo*" and back-translated as "friend" while the appropriate Spanish translation may have been "*amante*" (lover), "*conocido*" (acquaintance), or "*camarada*" (companion).

Another common problem with translators, and one particularly serious in the case of the double translation process, is the fact that good translators can usually make sense of badly translated versions. In this case, translators can produce a second original language version that is identical to the first one although the target language translation is of poor quality. The investigator may feel that the translation process has been properly carried out since the two original language versions are identical, but this may be the product of an avid and capable translator who was able to make sense of a poor translation into the target language.

A final limitation of the double translation approach is the fact that translators may keep the grammatical forms of the original language in producing the target language version. This very common problem among translators from English into Romance languages may aid in the production of an identical second version of the original language but may render the target language version incomprehensible or, at the least, stilted and awkward. An example of this problem occurs when translators utilize the passive tense of English in a language that is primarily active (such as Spanish). For example, the sentence "The idea was presented by John" may be translated keeping the passive tense "*La idea fué presentada por Juan*" rather than modifying it into a more appropriate (in Spanish) active tense "*Juan presentó la idea.*" The passive translation may produce an accurate second version in English but it may seem awkward in Spanish, introducing subtle differences in meaning that may be important in the research project.

In order to avoid some of the problems inherent in the double translation approach, the researcher may wish to implement the following steps:

> Besides being fully bilingual, translators should be bicultural so that they can understand the culture-specific nuances of the words utilized in the original language version and those to be used in the target language version.
>
> In carrying out the back translation from the target to the original language versions, translators should be explicitly told not to try to infer what

the original version may have said but rather to consider the target language version as the original version. Indeed, translators should be kept uninformed of the process (that is, whether they are the first or the second translator) in order to discourage any attempts at making sense of a poorly performed translation.

Interviewers should be made aware of the differences in language-specific tense (active or passive) and instructed to translate into the target language keeping in mind these differences.

Translators should be urged to identify words that could be translated in several ways so that connotative meanings can be elucidated.

Translators should be asked to identify items, words, or sentences that seem awkward in Spanish when translating back to English.

Decentering

This is a translation method that can be considered an extension of the double translation procedure in order to produce linguistic versions that are fully equivalent and culturally appropriate. Decentering was first proposed by Werner and Campbell (1970) as a way of developing instruments that would be culturally appropriate when cross-cultural research is conducted.

The basic assumption of decentering is that the original data-gathering instrument developed in one language is not considered finalized until the whole translation process has come to an end. The original language version that is given to the first translator in the double translation procedure becomes a draft of the instrument to be modified as the translation procedure evolves. This initial draft version is changed as the translation process shows that grammatical structures in the original version produced awkward or stilted versions in the target language or when it is clear that the concepts included in the original language version are inappropriate, unknown, or lack a verbal equivalent in the target language. As an outcome of this continuous comparison between both versions, modifications are introduced in the original language version to account for the characteristics or limitations of the target language.

A basic difference between double translation and decentering is that the latter considers both languages equally important in the production of the instrument while double translation considers the original language the standard against which the target version is to be compared. Decentering extends the length of the translation process because of the multiple translation iterations that are required; but it guarantees the production of not only culturally appropriate instruments but, more important, fully equivalent linguistic versions.

An example of item decentering might be a question that originally utilized the word "friend" in English to denote a live-in companion ("Does your friend share in household duties such as shopping and washing dishes?") The adequate translation into Spanish (given the appropriate context) would be "¿Comparte su amante las labores de la casa tales como las compras y el lavar los platos?" The English word "friend" would become "lover" in the back translation to English. Decentering the original question would imply changing it to "Does your lover share in household duties such as shopping and washing dishes?," a more appropriate and exact indication of what was initially meant.

A very telling example of the advantages of decentering is found in research conducted by Brislin (1980) with the Marlowe-Crowne Social Desirability Scale among the native residents of Guam and the Marianas Islands who speak Chamorro. As part of the translation and decentering process an item that originally read, "I like to gossip at times" became "I sometimes like to talk about other people's business" (Brislin, 1980). The main reason for the change is the fact that "gossip" did not translate well since Chamorro has different terms for male and female gossip while the word "gossip" in English does not specify the "gender" of the gossip.

In one of the few tests of the usefulness of decentering in producing instruments that are culturally appropriate, Schoua (1985) tested the reactions of three groups of Hispanics (Cubans, Mexican, and Argentinians) to two different versions of an instrument. One version had been double translated from English into Spanish and decentered while the second version was just double translated. As expected, the version that had been decentered as part of the double translation procedure was perceived as more appropriate than the version that was not decentered. The decentered version also was judged to be appropriate to all of the Hispanic subgroups by the respondents. In a different study (Cortese & Smyth, 1979), investigators found that decentering was useful in identifying questions in the original version that were ambiguous in meaning. Double translation with decentering solved problems in the wording of the scale and produced a more comprehensible data collection instrument in English and in Spanish.

Decentering has two significant disadvantages other than the already mentioned increase in time demanded by the procedure. Because of the conceptual modifications that may be required, the length of the text of the instrument being translated may be substantially increased. In some cases idiomatic expressions will need to be replaced by descriptive sentences and implicit cultural meaning will need to be made explicit. An additional disadvantage of this procedure is that instruments (such as IQ tests and personality scales) that have been normalized in the original language will need to be renormalized in the original language after being translated and decentered whenever modifications to question or item wording are introduced because the original norms are no longer valid (Cauce & Jacobson, 1980). Obviously this process of renormalization is expensive and time-consuming. Nevertheless, these disadvantages are offset by production of instruments that are fully comparable.

TRANSLATION PROBES

Given that all of the translation approaches mentioned above have limitations, researchers have developed translation probes that allow them to better estimate the accuracy and appropriateness of a given translation. These probes can be utilized in conjunction with the translation methods mentioned above and together should provide the investigator with a better understanding of the quality of the translation at hand. Some of these translation probes have been erroneously labeled translation methods by some authors and have been described as alternative ways of carrying out translations of text or instruments. We have chosen to call them translation probes since they all share the goal of testing the accuracy of the translation by comparing how closely the target language version is related to the original.

Field Pretest

This translation probe is carried out in order to test how accurately the connotative meaning of the instrument has been captured in the translated version. A group of individuals who resemble those targeted as part of the research project are asked to read or listen to the questions or items or sentences in a document one at a time and then to paraphrase them. Alternatively, the individuals being questioned as part of this translation probe can be asked to express their understanding of the item by answering a question such as "What do you think this question asks?"

The majority of the responses of the individuals surveyed in this fashion should closely resemble the ideas of the investigator when the questions or items were originally written. If there is a substantial number of discrepancies, the translation will need to be reviewed in order to identify why the translated item or question is being misinterpreted by the respondents. A possible outcome of this assessment may be that the format of the question in the original language may need to be revised and the item retranslated.

The field pretest procedure is particularly important when an instrument uses questions that can be answered with a yes or a no or by marking a point on a scale. Pretests with the instrument in which respondents are simply asked to answer the items may not indicate any problems since the expected responses are easily produced even when the respondent does not understand the question. Asking the respondents to verbalize the perceived meaning of each question or sentence will allow the investigators to know if the intended message or idea is being transmitted.

Use of Bilinguals

A second translation probe that has been utilized with some frequency consists of asking bilingual individuals to answer both language versions of the instrument (Prince & Mombour, 1967). The investigator then compares the responses given by the same individual to both linguistic versions, including testing for the significance of mean differences through statistical analyses. The expectation in this translation probe is that bilinguals should provide identical or very similar responses to an instrument when answering it in both languages. Any discrepancy in responses would be the result of a faulty translation of the instrument.

Although this translation probe is based on a conceptually appealing assumption (bilinguals producing similar responses to two linguistic versions of an instrument), research has shown that this expectation may be faulty. Ervin (1964) showed that bilinguals taking projective personality tests in English and in French provided different responses to the same stimuli depending on the language in which they took the test. Achievement responses for example, were common in English while verbal aggression and autonomy enhancing responses were more salient in French.

Some studies with Hispanics (Katerberg, Smith, & Hoy, 1977; Lubin, Natalicio, & Seever, 1985; Shorkey & Whiteman, 1978) have shown that bilinguals provide very similar responses when answering standard attitudinal and personality scales. Nevertheless, a study with young bilingual Hispanic children in New York (Findling, 1971) showed that when answering in English, these children responded with greater future orientation and need for affiliation than when they answered the same instrument in Spanish. An earlier study (Glatt, 1969) with a personality test (the MMPI) showed that bilinguals gave different responses to certain items depending on the language of administration and obtained scale scores that were higher in Spanish than in English. Part of the inconsistencies in these early studies may be due to differences in the quality of the translation of the instruments together with the fact that most of them did not appropriately control the level of bilingualism of the respondents.

A more recent study (Marín, Triandis, Betancourt, & Kashima, 1983) has shown that when answering a battery of emic (culture-specific) and etic (universal) items, Hispanic bilinguals of equivalent linguistic ability in both languages differed in their responses. These differences were found not only in terms of actual statistical differences to a significant proportion of the items (23%) but also in terms of different factor structures when the responses were submitted to separate (by language) factor analyses. The majority of the items where statistically significant responses were found were emic items that dealt with culturally appropriate ways of showing respect and dignity toward others. These items also had been judged as being highly socially desirable.

Given the above findings, researchers should generally avoid this translation probe. Differences in responses may be due to culture-specific values manifested through each language or to the social desirability of the items as perceived by bilinguals working in a specific language.

Performance Checks

If the instrument includes tasks to be performed by the respondents, the quality of the translation will be easier to ascertain since respondents of this probe must perform the expected behavior upon hearing or reading the request. In implementing this type of translation probe, a sample of individuals similar to the group targeted for study is asked to perform the tasks requested by each of the items in question. If an item demands that individuals place a set of cards in a given order and those included in the translation check actually carry out the task (barring performance differences due to levels of intelligence, unfamiliarity with the task, or physical disabilities), then the assumption of appropriate translation can be expected to be correct. Behaviors or performances that disagree with the content or request of the translated item usually indicate a translation problem.

Unfortunately, the majority of instruments utilized by social and behavioral scientists do not include behavioral requests that can be checked through this type of translation probe so that its practical usefulness is limited.

Evaluation by Experts

Another commonly used translation probe consists of having experts (colleagues, linguists, community leaders) evaluate the translated version of the instrument in terms of its linguistic appropriateness. These experts are asked to review the translated version and to identify items or questions that may be misunderstood or that are confusing to the average individual member of the target group. These experts can also provide feedback regarding the grammatical appropriateness of the translation as well as identify those words that may have various meanings or that are infrequently used in a given language or by some members of the group.

This procedure is extremely useful to identify regional or dialectical variations in vocabulary that may cause problems for the respondents. Extreme care should be used in the selection of the reviewers since their biases and personal linguistic experiences will be reflected in their comments. A recent study in Texas (Hendricson et al., 1989) utilized this approach as part of the translation of a health status questionnaire. Their experts were members of the target community who were familiar with Spanish and with Hispanic residents of rural communities. An evaluation of this approach showed that the final version of the instrument was well received by the target population.

Given the number of translation probes possible, investigators should carefully consider the most appropriate probe for the type of instrument that is being translated. The following steps are recommended:

The translated version of an instrument should be submitted to a thorough pretest that asks respondents to verbalize the connotative meaning of the various parts of the instrument through paraphrasing or through questions such as "What do you think this question asks?"

Given the variations in Spanish mentioned at the beginning of the chapter, researchers should include an evaluation of the translation by experts or consultants, including representatives from the major Hispanic subgroups: Central Americans, Cuban-Americans, Mexican-Americans, South Americans, and Puerto Ricans.

CHOOSING TRANSLATORS

The success of a translation depends heavily on the qualifications of the translators, but individuals who are not conversant with the target language will have difficulty evaluating a translator's skill. An individual is not necessarily a qualified translator simply by virtue of being a member of a given ethnic or national group (e.g., self-identifies as a Hispanic).

It should not be surprising that a person who can speak Spanish at home with parents or with friends may still not be qualified to carry out an appropriate translation of a text or instrument into Spanish. A recent immigrant may not have the appropriate educational level, familiarity with English and culture, or knowledge of regional variations in Spanish to be able to make an adequate translation. Hispanic graduate students or colleagues may understand Hispanic culture but may lack an appropriate understanding of Spanish; graduate students or professors of Spanish may understand the language but lack the required cultural sensitivity. Knowledge and experience are two key requirements that an investigator should look for in hiring a translator. Any research project should budget for the proper remuneration of qualified translators.

In budgeting translation costs, investigators can keep in mind that Brislin (1976) has found that translators can work effectively at a rate of 400 words per hour or about 2,400 to 3,000 words per day for technical or scientific materials. In budgeting for a research project, investigators should assume that research protocols and survey instruments will take at least twice as long as the above estimates.

In looking for translators, the investigator should consider the following suggestions:

When choosing translators, preference should be given to coordinate bilinguals (those who learned the languages at different times and, preferably, in two different cultures) over compound bilinguals (those who learned the languages at the same time). Coordinate bilinguals may be better able to articulate the cultural meaning of the words while compound bilinguals will perceive the text from the perspective of the one culture in which they learned both languages.

Experienced translators, while more costly than volunteers, will produce a higher quality product. References and samples of work should be required of all prospective translators.

Because the probability of errors increases with each retyping, the translator should produce a word-processed version that is compatible with the researcher's word-processing program and that includes diacritical marks (accents, tildes, and inverted question and exclamation marks).

Commercial translation services (advertised in magazines, newspapers or through the telephone directory) usually do not utilize these translation approaches since they are geared toward producing fast versions of commercial products. Researchers should be careful in contracting with these companies and request samples of scientific translations that the company may have produced.

As mentioned throughout this chapter, the translation of instruments and research protocols is without any doubt one of the most important steps in a study with respondents who do not speak English or who prefer to speak in their native or original language. While there are a number of possible translation procedures, all of them are subject to inaccuracies, making the translation process a delicate and at times frustrating activity. Researchers should become aware of the limitations of the various approaches mentioned above and make choices based on the potential accuracy of the translation approach to be used. Although time-consuming and expensive, a proper translation is essential to the usefulness of the results of a given study. It is said that Manuel Cervantes, who wrote *Don Quijote,* compared a translation to the back of a tapestry, meaning that a translation usually blurs the original picture and sometimes makes it impossible to see. We assume he was not using double translation with decentering.

6

Potential Problems in Interpreting Data

This final chapter covers some potential problems suggested by various researchers regarding the interpretation of data collected among Hispanics. For some time now, investigators have suggested that care needs to be taken when analyzing and interpreting Hispanic data because of concerns that Hispanics may often provide inaccurate and socially desirable responses, may produce large proportions of missing data, may prefer extreme and acquiescent responses, and may show low self-disclosure to strangers. This chapter will review the evidence available for each of these assumptions and will suggest ways in which researchers can deal with these plausible alternative explanations for their research findings. In reviewing the studies mentioned below, the reader needs to keep in mind that in many cases there is limited evidence for these assumptions. Often, the extent of the problems has not been appropriately documented.

EXTREME RESPONSE SETS

Various authors (e.g., Hui & Triandis, 1989) have suggested that Hispanics tend to prefer the use of extreme response categories in proportions that are higher than those found among non-Hispanic Whites. The results of these studies have shown that Hispanic respondents are less likely to use the middle response categories whenever presented with response scales that allow for moderating the answer to a question such as is the case in a 5-point Likert-type scale. Hispanics more often choose the extremes (e.g., Definitively True, Agree a Lot) on response scales than do non-Hispanic Whites, who would choose with equal probability the other response categories (e.g., "Probably True," "Agree a Little"). The existence of this response style can seriously affect the results of a study since group variances and score correlations can be affected by these extreme response styles.

A recent study with African-Americans (Bachman & O'Malley, 1984) showed that there was a definite preference for choosing extreme responses by Blacks as compared with non-Hispanic Whites. These response patterns were observed across various surveys conducted with graduating high school students from across the country. Based on this study, the argument has been made that Hispanics as well as other ethnic and racial minorities may also exhibit a preference for extreme response styles. The study by Hui and Triandis (1989) examined this assumption with a sample of 59 Hispanics and 60 non-Hispanics who were being assigned to jobs in the U.S. Navy. The respondents answered 165 items dealing with expected types of interpersonal relationships in work-related situations. In the study by Hui and Triandis, Hispanics were found to make more extreme responses than non-Hispanics but only when using 5-point Likert-type scales. When the responses to 10-point scales were analyzed, there were no ethnic differences in the choice of extreme responses.

Recently, we (Marín et al., in press) have studied this extreme response set with four large data sets that included responses by Hispanics ($N = 1,908$) and non-Hispanic Whites ($N = 14,425$) as well as a measure of acculturation. The analyses of the responses obtained in all four data sets showed that Hispanics consistently preferred extreme responses to a greater extent than did non-Hispanic Whites. Hispanics chose extreme responses to as many as 72% of the questions in one of the data sets, although there was significant variability across data sets (ranging from a low of 43% to a high of 72%). When the actual mean number of extreme responses was compared across ethnicities in each of the data sets, the results showed that Hispanics consistently made more extreme choices than non-Hispanic Whites. Overall, our analyses showed that there were no gender differences in the preference for extreme responses but that the less educated tended to make more extreme responses than the more highly educated (those with at least 12 years of formal education).

When the responses of Hispanics were studied for the possible role of acculturation in the preference for extreme responses, our analyses (Marín et al., in press) showed that overall, the less acculturated Hispanics preferred to make extreme choices in greater proportions than the more acculturated. These findings support the notion that extreme response sets are culture-specific response patterns. As a matter of fact, Hui and Triandis (1989) have suggested that certain cultures view extreme responses as more sincere. According to this cultural rule, the use of the middle categories of a response scale is a way of hiding a person's real feelings by presenting them in moderated terms (e.g., Somewhat Disagree).

While the existence of extreme response sets among Hispanics has only been confirmed in a few studies (Hui & Triandis 1989; Marín, et al., in press) researchers need to consider the possibility of this preference for extreme responses among Hispanics. As suggested by Bachman and O'Malley (1984), investigators analyzing data obtained from Hispanics should observe actual score distributions rather than just concentrating on measures of central tendency since extreme response sets may provide inaccurate descriptions of a group's responses if only measures of central tendency are considered. Furthermore, Bachman and O'Malley suggest that in analyzing multi-item scales with Hispanics, researchers may wish to explore alternative scoring methods where the extreme response is combined with a less-than-extreme response category. In this case, the researcher would not assign different scores to the two most extreme categories in a typical 5-point Likert scale. Rather, both the Agree and the Mostly Agree categories would be scored with the same value instead of assigning a higher score to Agree than to Mostly Agree. Triandis (personal communication, May 1990) has suggested that another alternative may be for the researcher to use standardized scores (z-scores) within respondents (if there are enough responses) or within instrument (if the items are homogeneous).

ACQUIESCENCE RESPONSE SETS

The acquiescence response set, or *yea-saying,* is a type of extreme response set in which respondents agree with statements presented to them or answer yes to questions regardless of their content. As was true for the extreme response set, acquiescence has seldom been studied among Hispanics but is often mentioned as a problem in data collection efforts.

One of the few studies dealing with acquiescence response sets among Hispanics was carried out by Ross and Mirowsky (1984) with 463 randomly selected non-Hispanic Whites and Mexican-Americans in El Paso, Texas, and a comparison group from Juárez, Mexico. Respondents were asked to answer a battery of psychological instruments including measures of social desirability, locus of control, and psychological distress. Their data showed that, overall, acquiescent responses were more likely to occur among men, among the aged, and among individuals of low socioeconomic status. The Mexican respondents from Juárez, Mexico, showed greater levels of acquiescent responses than the Mexican-Americans from El Paso, Texas, and than the non-Hispanic Whites.

An early study in Latin America (Landsberger & Saavedra, 1967) has shown that acquiescence is indeed frequent among Spanish-speakers but that it is closely related to educational level so that the less educated respondents are more likely to acquiesce than are the better educated. Other earlier studies with Hispanics in the United States have shown conflicting results. Gove (1977) found no differences in the proportion of acquiescent responses between Blacks, Hispanics, and non-Hispanic Whites in a survey of mental health status. On the other hand, Carr and Krause (1978) showed that Puerto Ricans were more likely to agree with a psychiatric symptom list than were non-Hispanic Whites. In a more recent study, Aday et al. (1980) found that the proportion of Hispanics showing acquiescence (24%) is higher than that found among the general population of the country (14%) when respondents are asked about their general health status.

Our recent study (Marín et al., in press) analyzing response sets among Hispanics found that indeed Hispanics were more likely to agree with a statement or to answer yes to a question than non-Hispanic Whites. As was true for the extreme response set, the less acculturated Hispanics tended to produce more acquiescent responses than the more highly acculturated respondents. Likewise, the less educated Hispanic respondents gave more acquiescent responses than the better educated, and there were no differences in rates of acquiescence among men and women. These findings were true across three of the four large data sets that were part of these secondary analyses. It should be noted, that although Hispanics are more likely to provide acquiescent responses, that type of response is provided to a relatively modest proportion of the questions, seldom reaching 50% of all questions.

Ross and Mirowsky (1984) have suggested that acquiescence can be perceived as a self-presentation strategy of individuals who are relatively powerless in society. In this sense, acquiescence becomes a deferential, submissive, and nonresistant response (Carr, 1971). By giving deferential responses, Ross and Mirowsky suggested, powerless people present "a good face" to the other members of society and may become more accepted. Indeed various studies cited by Ross and Mirowsky have shown an inverse relationship between socioeconomic status and the tendency to give acquiescent responses. Although their hypothesis is interesting and may explain the high rates of acquiescence among Hispanics in the United States, it does not necessarily fit with Ross and Mirowsky's own data that showed that Mexicans in Mexico showed greater levels of acquiescence than did Mexican-Americans residing in El Paso, Texas.

Tangential support for Ross and Mirowsky's (1984) assumption of acquiescent response styles being due to socioeconomic powerlessness on the part of the respondents can be found in the fact that in our analysis of four large data sets (Marín, et al., in press), the level of education of the respondents, usually associated with income, significantly affected the number of acquiescent responses made by Hispanics and by non-Hispanic Whites in most of the data sets. Nevertheless, the ethnicity of the respondents produced strong main effects in all data sets and, when educational level was controlled in the Hispanic data, the acculturation level of the Hispanic respondents showed significant main effects. These findings lend support to Hui and Triandis's (1989) notion that acquiescence and extreme response sets are moderated by the respondents' cultural values, Hispanic culture being one that promotes these response styles. A composite hypothesis could argue that extreme response sets are culturally determined although moderated by the respondents' educational level and by the extent of personal involvement with a given culture (acculturation). Our data (Marín et al., in press) seem to support this latter assumption although other studies should be conducted to test this hypothesis or other rival interpretations of the phenomenon.

SOCIALLY DESIRABLE RESPONSES

Closely related to the previous two response style sets is the observation that Hispanics often give socially desirable responses when participating in a survey or in some similar research project. For example, they may be more willing to report that they carry out socially desirable actions (e.g., voting, reading books, visiting relatives) but may avoid reporting less desirable attitudes or behaviors, (e.g., smoking, drinking alcoholic beverages in excess, having extramarital relationships). In this sense, researchers (e.g., Ross & Mirowsky, 1984) have argued that Hispanics exhibit a tendency to provide the "correct" answer, at least as perceived by the respondents, independent of the content of the question or of their actual experiences.

There are few published studies that have analyzed the effects of social desirability on Hispanics' responses. An early study on the mental health status of Puerto Rican migrants (Krause & Carr, 1978) showed that social desirability did not affect the rates of psychiatric symptomatology identified in the study.

The Ross and Mirowsky (1984) study that was described above tried to measure the frequency of socially desirable responses among Hispanics by using the well-known scale developed by Marlowe and Crowne. This instrument asks respondents to report if they carry out behaviors that are socially desirable but relatively uncommon (e.g., liking everybody or always helping those in need) and socially undesirable but relatively common (e.g., being jealous of another's luck or trying to get even rather than forgive). The data obtained by Ross and Mirowsky showed that the Mexican-American respondents were indeed more likely to express socially desirable answers than were the non-Hispanic Whites. Interestingly, the Mexicans residing in Mexico were more likely to express socially desirable responses than were the Mexican-Americans. Socioeconomic status also affected this tendency so that those respondents with lower socioeconomic status were more likely to express socially desirable answers than those better off economically.

Ross and Mirowsky (1984) explain their findings of greater frequency of socially desirable responses in terms of their hypothesis of nonresistant, deferential responding that is expected of those with low social power or prestige. The inverse correlation they found between socioeconomic status and social desirability could certainly be perceived as supporting this hypothesis. The alternative explanation of Marín and colleagues, (in press) suggesting the existence of a cultural value among Hispanics that encourages these responses in order to promote fluid social relations is equally tenable. This is particularly true when one considers the existence of the social script of *simpatía* among Hispanics (Triandis, Marín, Lisansky, & Betancourt, 1984) that specifically mandates politeness and respect and discourages criticism, confrontation, and assertiveness. Providing socially desirable answers could be a way to promote positive, smooth relationships between researcher and participant.

While the evidence for the tendency of Hispanics to provide socially desirable responses is limited and mixed, researchers may wish to consider this phenomenon when their research deals with topics that may lend themselves to socially desirable answers. One way in which researchers can control for social desirability is by including as part of their research protocol one of the scales developed for that purpose. Unfortunately, no single social desirability scale has been submitted to appropriate psychometric analyses with Hispanics although a number of unpublished translations exist. In our own research we have utilized the shorter version of the Marlowe-Crowne scale (Strahan & Gerbasi, 1972) when studying attitudes, values, and norms related to cigarette smoking and have found that the responses we measured were not affected by social desirability at least as measured by that scale.

INACCURATE REPORTING OF BEHAVIORS

The inaccurate reporting of behaviors that are perceived to be socially undesirable or counternormative has been widely documented in the literature for non-Hispanics. Recent studies have shown for example that, in general, there is a tendency to underreport cigarette consumption by adults (Warner, 1978) and by adolescent and young adults (Luepker, Pallonen, Murray, & Pirie, 1989). Other studies have found that underreporting also occurs for rates of consumption of alcoholic beverages (Poikolainen & Karkkainem, 1985), when reporting types of sexual behavior in which respondents may engage (Catania, McDermott, & Pollack, 1986; Saltzman, Stoddard, McCusker, Moon, & Mayer, 1987), and for reports of the consumption of illegal drugs (Mensch & Kandel, 1988). These response patterns, particularly for personally threatening questions, have usually been explained by researchers (e.g., Bradburn, Sudman, Blair, & Stocking, 1978) as an attempt to save face or to present a positive self-image to the interviewer and to others.

While the evidence for under- or overreporting among Hispanics is limited, some authors (Aday et al., 1980) have suggested that there is a tendency among Hispanics to report certain behaviors inaccurately. As a matter of fact, analyses of some data sets have shown inaccurate reporting by Hispanic respondents that could be interpreted as being the product of a need to provide socially desirable responses to threatening questions.

In an analysis of surveys of health care utilization, Aday et al. (1980) found that Hispanics tended to overestimate the number of visits made to a physician by 25% while non-Hispanics overestimated this behavior by 14%. In this study, responses to questionnaires were checked against records provided by physicians, hospitals, and third-party payers of health care (e.g., insurance companies, health maintenance organizations). In the same study, the number of hospital admissions was underestimated by Hispanics although non-Hispanics overestimated. Although the study is somewhat limited in terms of the actual comparability of the data, the results do show a possible tendency on the part of Hispanics to report certain behaviors inaccurately. Social desirability is a potential explanation for these responses since the respondents could perceive the underreporting of costly hospital admissions and the overreporting of preventive physician visits as socially desirable answers to a survey dealing specifically with patterns and costs of health care utilization, as was the case in the data analyzed by Aday and colleagues.

Two recent studies (Coultas, Howard, Peake, Skipper, & Samet, 1988; Pérez-Stable, Marín, Marín, Brody, & Benowitz, 1990) have analyzed discrepancies between self-reported smoking behavior and biochemical validation of cotinine levels among Hispanics. Cotinine is the principal metabolite of nicotine and is easily measured by well-established and reliable biochemical procedures. In the Coultas et al. (1988) study, a representative sample of New Mexico Hispanics was studied in order to establish prevalence of cigarette smoking. While 30.9% of the males self-reported being current smokers, 39.1% were actual smokers based on the biochemical validation procedures. There was a similar increase for women, for whom smoking prevalence by self-report was 27.1% but increased to 33.2% based on biochemical validation.

In our recent study (Pérez-Stable et al., 1990), we analyzed the responses of a random sample of 547 Mexican American smokers to a question in the H-HANES on the number of cigarettes smoked per day and compared their answers with a biochemical procedure that measures serum cotinine levels, allowing us to estimate the accuracy of the self-report. We found that 20.4% of the men and 24.7% of the women who reported smoking less than nine cigarettes per day were underreporting the number of cigarettes smoked in an average day. Nevertheless, this tendency to underreport was lower among those who reported smoking more cigarettes per day (8.3% for men smoking between 9 and 20 cigarettes per day). Interestingly, we found that the tendency to underreport was not related to the educational or acculturation level of the respondents.

As mentioned above, the evidence for a tendency among Hispanics to provide inaccurate responses is limited. Nevertheless, researchers should be aware of this possibility when planning data collection efforts. This response pattern may be particularly important to control in studies dealing with sensitive or personally threatening behaviors (e.g., sexual patterns, consumption of alcoholic beverages) or when the behavior in question may be socially rejected (e.g., cigarette smoking). Validation checks or measures of the reliability of the responses may be included in the study in order to better estimate the presence of under- or overreporting.

INCOMPLETE RESPONSES OR MISSING DATA

The possibility that Hispanics tend to give incomplete answers to questionnaires or that they tend to leave a large number of questions unanswered has been raised by some authors (e.g., Aday et al., 1980). The evidence for this response pattern among Hispanics is minimal but sufficiently important to warrant researchers' attention.

An early study with Hispanic migrant workers (Zusman & Olson, 1977) found that, in general, respondents left an average of 8% of the questions unanswered. Aday et al. (1980) in the study mentioned above dealing with patterns of utilization of health care facilities found that Hispanics had greater proportions of missing data (due to unanswered questions) than did non-Hispanics in two of the five areas studied in the questionnaire. The proportion of unanswered questions ranged from 0% to 1.9% for Hispanics compared with a range of 0.2% to 0.5% for non-Hispanic Whites. Interestingly, they found that the proportion of missing data among Hispanics was greater for those who answered the interview in Spanish (range of 0.1% to 5.9%) than among those who used English (range of 0% to 0.3%). In a recent study (Marín & Marín, 1989) comparing different interviewing approaches, we found that the ranges of missing data varied from 1% to 6% depending on the type of instrument utilized. These proportions are similar to those found among non-Hispanic respondents (Johnson & Delamater, 1976) when the topic of the survey is highly personal (e.g., sexual behavior).

Aday et al. (1980) suggested that the higher levels of missing data found among Hispanics could be explained by respondents' difficulty in understanding the concepts addressed by the items in the question-naire, especially since it was for the Spanish-speakers that a larger proportion of data were missing. Spanish-speaking Hispanics could be expected to be less acculturated than the English-speakers and therefore less likely to understand fully issues related to the delivery of health services in the United States. On the other hand, our data showing greater proportions of missing data for questions dealing with sexual behaviors could be interpreted as supporting the notion of social desirability and face-saving when answering threatening questions, a hypothesis that was mentioned above regarding the provision of inaccurate responses by Hispanics.

While the studies to date do not include a clear indication of the reasons or even of the extent of the problem, researchers should be aware of this potential difficulty when analyzing Hispanic data. Given that a large proportion of missing data can seriously affect the accuracy of statistical inferences, researchers should run initial analyses that identify rates of missing data by types of questions and by language of interview. Ideally, the proportions of missing data should be within the ranges usually found for non-Hispanic respondents. If this is not true, care should be taken in the interpretation and reporting of analyses where a significant proportion of the respondents have failed to provide answers.

LEVEL OF SELF-DISCLOSURE

Another factor that may affect the quality of the data collected among Hispanics is the level of self-disclosure that Hispanics are willing to provide a stranger. Various researchers have suggested that in general, Hispanics exhibit less self-disclosure than do non-Hispanic Whites (Dimond & Hellkamp, 1969; Gomez, 1987). These lower levels of self-disclosure could be assumed to decrease the validity of Hispanic responses since specific details or estimates of actual behavior could be ignored or hidden from the researcher by the research participant's unwillingness to self-disclose.

More recent studies have analyzed the variables that may affect the assumed unwillingness of Hispanics to self-disclose. LeVine and Franco (1981) found that Hispanics were less likely to self-disclose than non-Hispanic Whites in a variety of situations. Their questionnaire included different situations under which individuals may be willing to share personal information (for example, talking about tastes, money, or one's body to a male friend, a parent, or a spouse). Although both male and female Hispanics were generally unwilling to self-disclose in comparison to non-Hispanic Whites, Hispanic females reported being more likely to self-disclose to other women than were non-Hispanic women. Interestingly, while Hispanic males were the least willing to self-disclose, they expressed a willingness to self-disclose whenever the interviewer or researcher was a Hispanic female. In a subsequent study (Franco et al., 1984) the authors found that the acculturation level of the Hispanic respondents did not affect their level of reported self-disclosure.

While it is difficult to explain why Hispanics may be less likely to self-disclose than non-Hispanics, Franco and colleagues (1984) have suggested that Hispanics may be less willing to self-disclose to someone with whom they may interact in the future. This interpretation of their results fits with the cultural importance of face-saving and social desirability mentioned above. Another possibility is that Hispanics may be less willing to self-disclose in research contexts that are culturally alien. Evidence from psychotherapeutic situations shows that when the interaction between client and therapist was framed within a culturally appropriate context that valued the culture and history of Hispanics, adolescents were very willing to self-disclose (Constantino, Malgady, & Rogler, 1988).

Unwillingness to self-disclose is a methodological problem that is difficult for researchers to control. As suggested in Chapter 3, the use of Hispanic researchers and interviewers can enhance the sense of trust between participant and researcher and that in turn can be expected to enhance a participant's self-disclosure. Likewise, the involvement of Hispanic researchers can be expected to enhance the possibility of producing instruments that are culturally appropriate and these in turn may promote self-disclosure, as suggested by Constantino and colleagues (1988). As with all of the other problems in data collection mentioned in this chapter, researchers need to consider how the low levels of self-disclosure may affect the quality of the data collected with Hispanic respondents.

In summary, researchers should be aware of the possibility of a number of problems that may invalidate data collected from Hispanics. Among these are the tendency to provide extreme, acquiescent, or socially desirable responses; the possibility of responses not reflecting reality; and the presence of incomplete responses or of missing data. The experiences of various investigators suggest that the following steps should be taken while analyzing data on Hispanics:

> To control partially for the presence of extreme and acquiescent responses, researchers should analyze the frequency distributions of the responses, not just measures of central tendency.

When extreme or acquiescent responses may be present, investigators may wish to explore coding Likert-type scales in alternative ways that could control for these response sets. One possibility is scoring the two most extreme responses in the scale with the same value.

Given the possibility of socially desirable responses, investigators may wish to include one of the scales that measure social desirability as part of their protocol or to reword questions in order to avoid this response tendency.

Whenever socially undesirable behavior is being measured or when topics are highly personal, investigators may need to explore the possibility of validating the responses provided by the respondents through biochemical indicators (when possible) or through the use of reports by additional informants. Diaries and direct unobtrusive observations are other possible options together with the validation of data with existing files or information.

To assess the possibility of large proportions of missing data, investigators should run initial analyses of their data to identify questions that have inordinate amounts of missing data, controlling for language of interview and acculturation level of the respondents. The presence of missing data should be inspected before scales are constructed or descriptive analyses are performed.

To enhance self-disclosure, researchers may need to ensure that interviewers and members of the research staff do not interact with research participants from their own community since they may be recognized from past interactions. Furthermore, research staff should be chosen so that they match the ethnic characteristics of the participants. Most important, instruments must be culturally appropriate (see Chapter 4).

This chapter has provided a brief overview of some issues or problems that may affect the products of research efforts. Although evidence for the existence of these potential problems is limited to few studies, often with small samples, investigators will need to consider the possibility of controlling or considering the effects on their studies of the issues discussed here. We have tried to include those areas that have caused concern to researchers collecting data from Hispanics, while being aware that the support for those assumptions is limited. In doing this, we hoped to forewarn researchers of pitfalls they may encounter when conducting research with Hispanics. We hope that the sheer number of issues discussed in this chapter will not discourage researchers from doing research with Hispanics. As the Spanish saying goes, *mas vale prevenir que lamentar* (it's better to prevent than to lament).

References

Acosta-Belén, E. (1988). From settlers to newcomers: The Hispanic legacy in the United States. In E. Acosta-Belén &. B. R. Sjostrom (Eds.), *The Hispanic experience in the United States: Contemporary issues and perspectives* (pp. 81-106). New York: Praeger.

Adams, B. N. (1974). Doing survey research cross-culturally: Some approaches and problems. *Journal of Marriage and the Family,* (August), 568-573.

Adams-Equivel, H., & Lang, D. A. (1987). The reliability of telephone penetration estimates in specialized target groups: The Hispanic case. *Journal of Data Collection, 27,* 35-39.

Aday, L. A., Chiu, G. Y., & Andersen, R. (1980). Methodological issues in health care surveys of the Spanish heritage population. *American Journal of Public Health, 70,* 367-374.

Advertisers study Hispanic values. (1989) *Hispanic Business, 11* (8), 50.

Alva, S. A. (1985). Political acculturation of Mexican American adolescents. *Hispanic Journal of Behavioral Sciences, 7* 345-364.

Alvirez, D., & Bean, F. D. (1976). The Mexican American family. In C. H. Mindel & R. N. Haberstein (Ed.), *Ethnic families in America* (pp. 271-291). New York: Elsevier.

Amaro, H. (1988). Women in the Mexican-American community: Religion, culture, and reproductive attitudes and experiences. *Journal of Community Psychology, 16,* 6-20.

Anderson, B. A., Silver, B. D., & Abramson, P. R. (1988). The effects of the race of the interviewer on race-related attitudes of Black respondents in SRC/CPS national election studies. *Public Opinion Quarterly, 52,* 289-324.

Baca Zinn, M. (1979). Field research in minority communities: Ethical, methodological, and political observations by an outsider. *Social Problems, 27,* 209-219.

Bachman, J. G., & O'Malley, P. M. (1984). Yea-saying, nay-saying, and going to extremes: Black-White differences in response styles. *Public Opinion Quarterly, 48,* 491-509.

Ball, J. C., & Pabon, D. O. (1965). Locating and interviewing narcotic addicts in Puerto Rico. *Sociology and Social Research, 49,* 401-411.

Barry, H. (1980). Description and uses of the Human Relations Area Files. In H. C. Triandis & J. W. Berry (Eds.), *Handbook of cross-cultural psychology* (pp. 445-478). Boston: Allyn & Bacon.

Bejar Navarro, R. (1986). *El mexicano: Aspectos culturales y psico-sociales.* Mexico: Universidad Nacional Autónoma de México.

Bengston, V. L., Grigsby, E., Corry, E. M., & Hruby, M. (1977). Relating academic research to community concerns: A case study in collaborative effort. *Journal of Social Issues, 33*(4), 75-92.

Berkanovic, E. (1980). The effects of inadequate language translation on Hispanics' responses to health surveys. *American Journal of Public Health, 70,* 1273-1276.

Bernal, M. E., North, J. A., Rosen, P. M., Delfini, L. F., & Schultz, L. A. (1979). Observer ethnicity effects on Chicano mothers and sons. *Hispanic Journal of Behavioral Sciences, 1,* 151-164.

Berry, J. W. (1969). On cross-cultural comparability. *International Journal of Psychology, 4* 207-229.

Berry, J. (1980). Acculturation as varieties of adaptation. In A. M. Padilla (Ed.), *Acculturation: Theory, models, and some new findings* (pp. 9-25) Boulder, CO: Westview.

Bird, H. R., Canino, G. J., & Shrout, P. E. (1985). *Considerations on the use of the mini-mental state examination within the Spanish Diagnostic Interview Schedule.* Paper presented at the meeting of the American Psychiatric Association, Dallas, TX.

Blauner, R., & Wellman, D. (1973). Toward the decolonization of social research. In J. A. Ladner (Ed.), *The death of white sociology.* New York: Vintage.

Bloom, D., & Padilla, A. M. (1979). A peer interviewer model in conducting surveys among Mexican American youth. Journal of Community Psychology, 7, 129-136.

Bradburn, N. M., Sudman, S., Blair, E., & Stocking, C. (1978). Question threat and response bias. *Public Opinion Quarterly, 42,* 221-234.

Brewer, R. E. & Brewer, M. B. (1971). Expressed evaluation toward a social object as a function of label. *Journal of Social Psychology, 84,* 257-260.

Brislin, R. W. (1970). Back translation for cross-cultural research. *Journal of Cross-Cultural Psychology, 1,* 185-216.

Brislin, R. W. (1976). *Translation: Applications and research.* New York: Gardner.

Brislin, R. W. (1980). Translation and content analysis of oral and written materials. In H. C. Triandis & J. W. Berry (Eds.), *Handbook of cross-cultural psychology* (pp. 389-444). Boston: Allyn & Bacon.

Brislin, R. W. (1986). The wording and translation of research instruments. In W. J. Lonner & J. W. Berry (Eds.), *Field methods in cross-cultural research* (pp. 137-164). Beverly Hills, CA: Sage.

Brislin, R. W., Lonner, W. J. & Thorndike, R. M. (1973). *Cross-cultural research methods.* New York: John Wiley.

Brown, E. D., & Sechrest, L. (1980). Experiments in cross-cultural research. In H. C. Triandis & J. E. Berry (Eds.). *Handbook of cross-cultural psychology* (pp. 297-318). Boston: Allyn & Bacon.

Bureau of the Census. (1973). *Persons of Spanish origin in the United States. March 1972 and 1971* (Technical Paper No. 250). Washington, DC: Government Printing Office.

Bureau of the Census. (1979). *Consistency of reporting of ethnic origin in the current population survey* (Technical Paper No. 31). Washington, DC: Government Printing Office.

Bureau of the Census. (1980). *Spanish surname list technical documentation* Washington, DC: Government Printing Office.

Bureau of the Census. (1982). *Persons of Spanish Origin by state: 1980* (Report PC80-S1-7). Washington, DC: Government Printing Office.

Bureau of the Census. (1983). *Ancestry of the population by state: 1980* (Supplementary Report PC80-S1-10). Washington, DC: Government Printing Office.

Bureau of the Census. (1986). *Projections of the Hispanic population: 1983-2080* (Current Population Reports, Series P-25, No. 995). Washington, DC: Government Printing Office.

Bureau of the Census. (1988). *The Hispanic population in the United States: March 1988* (Series P-20, No. 431) Washington, DC: Government Printing Office.

Bureau of the Census. (1989). *Population estimates by race and Hispanic origin for states, metropolitan areas and selected counties.* (Current Population Reports, Series P-25, No. 1040-RD-1). Washington, DC: Government Printing Office.

Burgoyne, R. W., Wolkon, G., & Staples, F. (1977). Do Latinos and Blacks participate in outpatient services consumer surveys? In E. R. Padilla & A. M. Padilla (Eds.), *Trans-cultural psychiatry: An Hispanic perspective.* Los Angeles: University of California, Spanish Speaking Mental Health Research Center.

Burnam, M. A., Telles, C. A., Karno, M., Hough, R. L., & Escobar, J. I. (1987). Measurement of acculturation in a community population of Mexican Americans. *Hispanic Journal of Behavioral Sciences, 9,* 105-130.

Caetano, R. (1986/1987). Drinking and Hispanic-American family life. *Alcohol Health & Research World, 11*(2), 26-34.

Carballo-Diéguez, A. (1989). Hispanic culture, gay male culture, and AIDS: Counseling implications. *Journal of Counseling and Development, 68*(September/October), 26-30.

Carr, L. (1971). The Srole items and acquiescence. *American Sociological Review, 36,* 287-293.

Carr, L., & Krause, N. (1978). Social status, psychiatric symptomatology, and response bias. *Journal of Health and Social Behavior, 19,* 86-91.

Castro, F. G. & Baezconde-Garbanati, L. (1987). *A schema for greater specificity in sampling from Latino populations.* Paper presented at the convention of the American Public Health Association, New Orleans, LA.

Catania, J. A., McDermott, L. J., & Pollack, L. M. (1986). Questionnaire response bias and face-to-face interview sample bias in sexuality research. *Journal of Sex Research, 22,* 52-72.

Cauce, A. M., & Jacobson, L. I. (1980). Implicit and incorrect assumptions concerning the assessment of the Latino in the United States. *American Journal of Community Psychology, 8,* 571-586.

Centers for Disease Control. (1987). Cigarette smoking among Black and other minority populations. *Mortality and Morbidity Weekly Report, 36*(25), 404-407.

Cohen, R. (1979). *Culture, disease and stress among Latino immigrants. Washington, DC: Smithsonian Institution.*

Constantino, G., Malgady, R. G., & Rogler, L. H. (1988). Folk hero modeling therapy for Puerto Rican adolescents. *Journal of Adolescence, 11,* 155-165.

Cortese, M., & Smyth, P. (1979). A note on the translation to Spanish of a measure of acculturation. *Hispanic Journal of Behavioral Sciences, 1,* 65-68.

Cotter, P. R. (1982). Race-of-interviewer effects in telephone interviewers. *Public Opinion Quarterly, 46,* 278-284.

Coultas, D. B., Howard, C. A. Peake, G. T., Skipper, B.J., & Samet, J. M. (1988). Discrepancies between self-reported and validated cigarette smoking in a community survey of New Mexico Hispanics. *American Review of Respiratory Disorders, 137,* 810-814.

Cromwell, R. E., & Ruiz, R. A. (1979). The myth of macho dominance in decision making with Mexican and Chicano families. *Hispanic Journal of Behavioral Sciences, 1,* 355-373.

Cuellar, I., Harris, L. C., & Jasso, R. (1980). An acculturation scale for Mexican American normal and clinical populations. *Hispanic Journal of Behavioral Sciences, 2* 199-217.

Davis, C., Haub, C., & Willette, J. (1983). U.S. Hispanics: Changing the face of America. *Population Bulletin, 38*(3), 1-44.

De Barbenza, C. M., & Montoya, O. A. (1979). Sobre la necesidad de efectuar adaptaciones regionales del MMPI. *Interamerican Journal of Psychology, 13,* 63-71.

Deyo, R. A. (1984). Pitfalls in measuring the health status of Mexican Americans: Comparative validity of the English and Spanish Sickness Impact Profile. *American Journal of Public Health, 74,* 569-573.

Deyo, R. A., Diehl, A. K., Hazuda, H., & Stern, M. P. (1985). A simple language-based acculturation scale for Mexican Americans: Validation and application to health care research. *American Journal of Public Health, 75,* 51-55.

Diaz-Guerrero, R. (1982). *Psicología del mexicano* (4th ed.). Mexico: Trillas.

Diaz-Guerrero, R., & Peck, R. F. (1963). *Respeto y posición social en dos culturas.* Paper presented at the Seventh Interamerican Congress of Psychology, Mexico City.

Dimond, R. E., & Hellkamp, D. T. (1969). Race, sex, ordinal position of birth, and self-disclosure in high school students. *Psychological Reports, 25,* 235-238.

Doi, T. L. (1973). *The anatomy of dependence.* Tokyo: Kodansha International.

Ervin, S. M. (1964). Language and TAT content in bilinguals. *Journal of Abnormal and Social Psychology, 68,* 500-507.

Escobedo, L. G., & Remington, P. L. (1989). Birth cohort analysis of prevalence of cigarette smoking among Hispanics in the United States. *Journal of the American Medical Association, 261,* 66-69.

Fairchild, H. H., & Cozens, J. A. (1981). Chicano, Hispanic or Mexican American: What's in a name? *Hispanic Journal of Behavioral Sciences, 3,* 191-198.

Federal Register. (1978, May 4). Washington, DC: Government Printing Office.

Feldman, R. E. (1968). Response to compatriot and foreigner who seek assistance. *Journal of Personality and Social Psychology, 10,* 202-214.

Fellows, M. R. (1979). *Irish Americans: Identity and assimilation.* Englewood Cliffs, NJ: Prentice-Hall.

Fetterman, D. M. (1989). *Ethnography: Step by step.* Newbury Park, CA: Sage.

Findling, J. (1971). Bilingual need affiliation and future orientation in extra-group and intra-group domains. In J. A. Fishman, R. L. Cooper, & R. Ma (Eds.), *Bilingualism in the barrio.* Bloomington: Indiana University Press.

Fishman, J. A. (1987). What is happening to Spanish on the U.S. mainland? *Ethnic Affairs, 1,*12-23.

Flaherty, J. A. (1987). Appropriate and inappropriate research methodologies for Hispanic mental health. In M. Gaviria & J. D. Arana (Eds.), *Health and behavior: Research agenda for Hispanics (pp. 177-186). Chicago: University of Illinois, Simon Bolivar Hispanic-American Psychiatric Research and Training Program.*

Fowler, F. J. (1988). *Survey research methods.* Newbury Park, CA: Sage.

Franco, J. N., Malloy, T., & Gonzalez, R. (1984). Ethnic and acculturation differences in self-disclosure. *Journal of Social Psychology, 122,* 21-32.

Freeman, D. M. (1969). A note on interviewing Mexican-Americans. *Social Science Quarterly, 49,* 909-918.

Frey, J. H. (1983). *Survey research by telephone.* Beverly Hills, CA: Sage.

Fromm, E., & Maccoby, M. (1973). *Sociopsicoanálisis del campesino mexicano.* Mexico: Fondo de Cultura Económica.

Gallimore, R., Weiss, L., & Finney, R. (1974). Cultural differences in delay of gratification: A problem of behavior classification. *Journal of Personality and Social Psychology, 30,* 72-80.

Garcia, J. (1972, September). IQ: The conspiracy. *Psychology Today,* pp. 42-43.

García Sevilla, L., Pérez, J., & Tobena, A. (1979). Fiabilidad y validez de la versión castellana del EPI. *Revista Latinoamericana de Psicología,, 11,* 393-402.

Garza, R. T. (1977). Personal control and fatalism in Chicanos and Anglos: Conceptual and methodological issues. In J. L. Martinez (Ed.), *Chicano psychology* (pp. 97-108). New York: Academic Press.

Giachello, A. L., Bell, R. Aday, L. A., & Anderson, R. M. (1983). Uses of the 1980 Census for Hispanic health service research. *American Journal of Public Health, 73,* 266-274.

Glatt, K. M. (1969). An evaluation of the French, Spanish and German translations of the MMPI. *Acta Psychologica, 29,* 65-84.

Glazer, N., & Moynihan, D. P. (1963). *Beyond the melting pot.* Cambridge: Harvard-MIT Press.

Godoy, H. (1976). *El carácter chileno.* Santiago, Chile: Editorial Universitaria.

Gomez, E. A. (1987). Hispanic Americans: Ethnic shared values and traditional treatment. *American Journal of Social Psychiatry, 7,* 215-219.

González Valdés, T. L. (1979). Estudio valorativo de algunas características del MMPI en pacientes con trastornos psíquicos. *Revista del Hospital Psiquiá)trico de La Habana, 20,* 249-258.

Good, B. J., & Good, M. J. (1986). The cultural context of diagnosis and therapy: A view from medical anthropology. In M. R. Miranda & H. H. Kitano (Eds.), *Mental health research and practice in minority communities: Development of culturally sensitive training programs* (pp. 1-27). Washington, DC: National Institute of Mental Health.

Gove, W. R. (1977). Response bias in survey of mental health: An empirical investigation. *American Journal of Sociology, 82,* 1289-1317.

Graves, D. T. (1967). Acculturation, access, and alcohol in a tri-ethnic community. *American Anthropologist, 69,* 306-321.

Grebler, L., Moore, J. W., & Guzman, R. C. (1970). *The Mexican American people.* New York: Free Press.

Griffith, J., & Villavicencio, S. (1985). Relationships among acculturation, sociodemographic characteristics and social support in Mexican American adults. *Hispanic Journal of Behavioral Sciences, 7,* 75-92.

Guarnaccia, P. J., Angel, R., & Worobey, J. L. (1989). The factor structure of the CES-D in the Hispanic Health and Nutrition Examination Survey: The influence of ethnicity, gender and language. *Social Science and Medicine. 29.* 85-94.

Gunther, H. (1981). Uma tentative de traduzir e adaptar a Escala de Valores de Rokeach para uso no Brasil. *Arquivos Brasileiros de Psicologia, 33*(3), 58-72.

Hall, E. T. (1969). *The hidden dimension.* Garden City, NY: Doubleday.

Hall, E. T. (1983). *The dance of life.* Garden City, NY: Anchor Books.

Hayes-Bautista, D. E. (1980). Identifying "Hispanic" populations: The influence of research methodology upon public policy. *American Journal of Public Health, 70,* 353-356.

Hayes-Bautista, D. E. (1983). On comparing studies of different Raza populations. *American Journal of Public Health, 73,* 274-276.

Hayes-Bautista, D. E. & Chapa, J. (1987). Latino terminology: Conceptual bases for standardized terminology. *American Journal of Public Health, 77,* 61-68.

Heller, C. S. (1966). *Mexican-American youth: Forgotten youth at the crossroads.* New York: Random House.

Hendricson, W. D., Russell, I. J., Prihoda, T. J., Jacobson, J. M., Rogan, A., & Bishop, G. D. (1989). An approach to developing a valid Spanish language translation of a health-status questionnaire. *Medical Care, 27,* 959-966.

Henggeler, S. W. & Tavormina, J. B. (1979). Stability of psychological assessment measures for children of Mexican American migrant workers. *Hispanic Journal of Behavioral Sciences, 1,* 263-270.

Henry, G. (1990). *Practical sampling.* Newbury Park, CA: Sage.

Hirsch, H. (1973). Political scientists and other camaradas: Academic myth making and racial stereotypes. In R. O. de la Garza, Z. A. Kruswski, & T. A. Arcinego (Eds.), *Chicanos and Native Americans* Englewood Cliffs, NJ: Prentice-Hall.

Hispanic almanac. (1984). Washington, DC: Author.

Hofstede, G. (1980). *Culture's consequences.* Beverly Hills, CA: Sage.

Holtzman, W. H., Diaz-Guerrero, R., & Swartz, J. D. (1975). *Personality development in two cultures.* Austin: University of Texas Press.

Howard, C. A., Samet, J. M., Buechley, R. W., Schrag, S. D., & Key, C. R. (1983). Survey research in New Mexico Hispanics: Some methodological issues. *American Journal of Epidemiology, 117,* 27-34.

Hui, C. H., & Triandis, H. C. (1989). Effects of culture and response format on extreme response style. *Journal of Cross-Cultural Psychology, 20,* 296-309.

Humm-Delgado, D., & Delgado, M. (1985). Gaining community entree to assess service needs of Hispanics. *Social Casework, 67*(2), 80-89.

Johnson, W. T., & Delamater, J. D. (1976). Response effects in sex surveys. *Public Opinion Quarterly, 40,* 165-181.

Jorgensen, D. L. (1989). *Participant observation: A methodology for human studies.* Newbury Park, CA : Sage.

Josephson, E. (1970). Resistance to community surveys. *Social Problems, 18,* 117-129.

Kagan, S., Knight, G. P., & Martinez-Romero, S. (1982). Culture and the development of conflict resolution style. *Journal of Cross-Cultural Psychology, 13,* 43-59.

Kagan, S., & Madsen, M. (1971). Cooperation and competition of Mexican, Mexican American, and Anglo American children of two ages under four instructional sets. *Developmental Psychology, 5,* 32-39.

Katerberg, R., Smith, F. J., & Hoy, S. (1977). Language, time, and person effects on attitude scale translations. *Journal of Applied Psychology, 62,* 385-391.

Kluckhohn, C., & Strodtbeck, F. L. (1961). *Variations in value orientations.* Westport, CT: Greenwood.

Knoll, T. (1982). *Becoming American.* Portland, OR: Coast-to-Coast.

Krause, N., & Carr, L. G. (1978). The effects of response bias in the survey assessment of the mental health of Puerto Rican migrants. *Social Psychiatry, 13*(3), 167-173.

Landsberger, H. A., & Saavedra, A. (1967). Response set in developing countries. *Public Opinion Quarterly, 31,* 214-229.

Lega, L. I. (1981). A Colombian version of the Children's Embedded Figures Test. *Hispanic Journal of Behavioral Sciences, 3,* 415-417.

Leite, D. M. (1976). *O Carater nacional brasileiro.* São Paulo: Livraria Pioneira Editora.

LeVine, E., & Franco, J. N. (1981). A reassessment of self-disclosure patterns among Anglo Americans and Hispanics. *Journal of Counseling Psychology, 28,* 522-524.

LeVine, E. S., & Padilla, A. M. (1980). *Crossing cultures in therapy: Pluralistic counseling for the Hispanic.* Belmont, CA: Brooks/Cole.

Levine, R. V., West, L. J., & Reis, H. T. (1980). Perceptions of time and punctuality in the United States and Brazil. *Journal of Personality and Social Psychology, 38,* 541-550.

Lindzey, G. (1961). *Projective techniques and cross-cultural research.* New York: Appleton-Century-Crofts.

López de Mesa, L. (1975). *De como se ha formado la nacón colombiana*. Medellín: Bedout.

Lubin, B., Natalicio, L., & Seever, M. (1985). Performance of bilingual subjects on Spanish and English versions of the Depression Adjective Checklist. *Journal of Clinical Psychology, 41*, 218-219.

Luepker, R. V., Pallonen, U. E., Murray, D. M., & Pirie, P. L. (1989). Validity of telephone surveys in assessing cigarette smoking in young adults. *American Journal of Public Health, 79*, 202-204.

Madsen, W. (1961). *Society and health in the Lower Rio Grande Valley*. Austin, TX: Hogg Foundation for Mental Health.

Maguire, J. F. (1969). *The Irish in America*. New York: Arno.

Malgady, R. G., Rogler, L. H., & Constantino, G. (1987). Ethnocultural and linguistic bias in mental health evaluation of Hispanics. *American Psychologist, 42*, 228-234.

Mannino, F. V., & Shore, M. F. (1976). Perceptions of social support by Spanish-speaking youth with implications for program development. *Journal of School Health, 46*, 471-474.

Marín, B. V., Marín, G., Pérez-Stable, E. J., Otero-Sabogal, R., & Sabogal, F. (1990). Cultural differences in attitudes toward smoking: Developing messages using the theory of reasoned action. *Journal of Applied Social Psychology, 20*, 478-493.

Marín, G. (1984). Stereotyping Hispanics: The differential effect of research method, label and degree of contact. *International Journal of Intercultural Relations, 8*, 17-27.

Marín, G. (1986). Consideraciones metodológicas básicas para conducir investigaciones psicológicas en América Latina. *Acta Psiquiátrica y Psicológica de América Latina, 32*, 183-192.

Marín, G. (1987). Attributions for tardiness among Chilean and United States students. *Journal of Social Psychology, 127*, 69-75.

Marín, G., Gamba, R. J., & Marín, B. V. (in press). Acquiescence and extreme response sets among Hispanics: The role of acculturation and education. *Journal of Cross-Cultural Psychology*.

Marín, G., & Marín, B. V. (1989). Comparison of three interviewing approaches for studying sensitive topics with Hispanics: Refusal rates, interviewee discomfort and perceived accuracy. *Hispanic Journal of Behavioral Sciences, 11*, 330-340.

Marín, G., Marín, B. V., Otero-Sabogal, R., Sabogal, F., & Pérez-Stable, E. J. (1989). The role of acculturation on the attitudes, norms and expectancies of Hispanic smokers. *Journal of Cross-Cultural Psychology, 20*, 399-415.

Marín, G., Marín, B. V., & Pérez-Stable, E. J. (1990). Feasibility of a telephone survey to study a minority community: Hispanics in San Francisco. *American Journal of Public Health, 80*, 323-326.

Marín, G., Marín, B. V., Pérez-Stable, E. J., Sabogal, F., & Otero-Sabogal, R. (1990). Changes in information as a function of a culturally appropriate smoking cessation community intervention for Hispanics. *American Journal of Community Psychology, 17*.

Marín, G., Pérez-Stable, E. J., & Marín, B. V. (1989). Cigarette smoking among San Francisco Hispanics: The role of acculturation and gender. *American Journal of Public Health, 79*, 196-198.

Marín, G., Pérez-Stable, E. J., Otero-Sabogal, R., Sabogal, F., & Marín, B. V. (1989). Stereotypes of smokers held by Hispanic and White non-Hispanic smokers. *International Journal of the Addictions, 24*, 203-213.

Marín, G., Sabogal, F., Marín, B. V., Otero-Sabogal, R., & Pérez-Stable, E. J. (1987). Development of a short acculturation scale for Hispanics. *Hispanic Journal of Behavioral Sciences, 9,* 183-205.

Marín, G., & Triandis, H. C. (1985). Allocentrism as an important characteristic of the behavior of Latin Americans and Hispanics. In R. Díaz-Guerrero (Ed.), *Cross-cultural and national studies in social psychology* (pp. 85-104). Amsterdam: Elsevier Science Publishers.

Marín, G., Triandis, H. C., Betancourt, H. & Kashima, Y. (1983). Ethnic affirmation versus social desirability: Explaining discrepancies in bilinguals' responses to a questionnaire.*Journal of Cross-Cultural Psychology, 14,* 173-186.

Marks, G., Solis, J., Richardson, J. L., Collins, L. M., Birba, L., & Hisserich, J. C. (1987). Health behavior of elderly Hispanic women: Does cultural assimilation make a difference? *American Journal of Public Health, 77,* 1315-1319.

Marsella, A. J. (1978). Thoughts on cross-cultural studies on the epidemiology of depression. *Cultural and Medical Psychiatry, 2,* 343-357.

McAlister, A. L., Amezcua, C. V., Ramirez, A. G., Stern, M. P., Galavotti, C. E., McCuan, R. A., & Hazuda, H. P. (in press). Three-year panel study of health promotion and smoking cessation in Southwest Texas border communities. *American Journal of Public Health.*

Mensch, B. S., & Kandel, D. B. (1988). Underreporting of substance use in a national longitudinal youth cohort: Individual and interviewer effects. *Public Opinion Quarterly, 52,* 100-124.

Merton, R. K. (1972). Insiders and outsiders: A chapter in the sociology of knowledge. *American Journal of Sociology, 78,* 9-48.

Mittlebach, F. G., & Moore, J. W. (1968). Ethnic endogamy—the case of the Mexican Americans. *American Journal of Sociology, 74,* 50-62.

Moore, J. W. (1970). *Mexican-Americans.* Englewood Cliffs, NJ: Prentice-Hall.

Moore, J. W. (1973). Social constraints on sociological knowledge: Academics and research concerning minorities. *Social Problems, 21,* 65-77.

Moskos, C. C. (1980). *Greek Americans.* Englewood Cliffs, NJ: Prentice-Hall.

National Center for Health Statistics. (1985). *Plan and operation of the Hispanic Health and Nutrition Examination Survey, 1982-1984 (PHS 85-1321). Washington, DC: Government Printing Office.*

Nelson, W., Knight, G. P., Kagan, S., & Gumbiner, J. (1980). Locus of control, self-esteem, and field independence as predictors of school achievement among Anglo American and Mexican American children. *Hispanic Journal of Behavioral Sciences, 2,* 323-335.

Newton, F. C., Olmedo, E. L., & Padilla, A. M. (1982). *Hispanic mental health research: A reference guide.* Berkeley: University of California Press.

Olmedo, E. L., Martinez, J. L. & Martinez, S. R. (1978). Measure of acculturation for Chicano adolescents. *Psychological Reports, 42,* 159-170.

O'Rourke, D., & Blair, J. (1983). Improving random respondent selection in telephone surveys. *Journal of Marketing Research, 23,* 428-432.

Padilla, A. M. (1980). The role of cultural awareness and ethnic loyalty in acculturation. In A. M. Padilla (Ed.), *Acculturation: Theory, models and some new findings* (pp. 47-84). Boulder, CO: Westview.

Padilla, E. R., Padilla, A. M., Ramirez, R., Morales, A. & Olmedo, E. L. (1979). Inhalent, marihuana, and alcohol abuse among barrio children and adolescents. *International Journal of the Addictions, 14,* 943-964.

Pérez-Stable, E. J. (1987). Issues in Latino health care. *Western Journal of Medicine, 146,* 213-218.

Pérez-Stable, E. J., Marín, B. V., Marín, G., Brody, D. J., & Benowitz, N. L. (1990). Apparent underreporting of cigarette consumption among Mexican American smokers. *American Journal of Public Health, 80,* 1057-1061.

Poikolainen, K., & Karkkainem, P. (1985). Nature of questionnaire options affects estimates of alcohol intake. *Journal of Studies on Alcohol, 46,* 219-222.

Portes, A., & Bach, R. L. (1985). *Latin journey: Cuban and Mexican immigrants in the United States.* Berkeley: University of California Press.

Potok, C. (1978). *Wanderings.* New York: Knopf.

Prince, R., & Mombour, W. (1967). A technique for improving linguistic equivalence in cross-cultural surveys. *International Journal of Social Psychiatry, 13,* 229-237.

Ramírez, S. (1977). *El mexicano: Psicología de sus motivaciones.* Mexico: Grijalbo.

Rendon, A. B. (1971). *Chicano manifesto.* New York: Macmillan.

Reschly, D. J. (1978). Factor structures among Anglos, Blacks, Chicanos, and Native-American Papagos. *Journal of Consulting and Clinical Psychology, 46,* 417-422.

Rogg, E. M. (1974). *The assimilation of Cuban exiles: The role of community and class.* New York: Aberdeen.

Rogler, L. H. (1989). The meaning of culturally sensitive research in mental health. *American Journal of Psychiatry, 146,* 296-303.

Rogler, L. H., & Hollingshead, A. B. (1985). *Trapped: Puerto Rican families and schizophrenia.* Maplewood, NJ: Waterfront.

Rogler, L. H., Malgady, R. G., & Rodriguez, O. (1989). *Hispanics and mental health: A framework for research.* Malabar, FL: Robert E. Krieger Publishing.

Ross, C. E., & Mirowsky, J. (1984). Socially-desirable response and acquiescence in a cross-cultural survey of mental health. *Journal of Health and Social Behavior, 25,* 189-197.

Ryan, E. B., & Carranza, M. A. (1976). Ingroup and outgroup reactions to Mexican American language varieties. In H. Giles (Ed.), *Language, ethnicity and intergroup relations.* New York: Academic Press.

Sabogal, F., Marín, G., Otero-Sabogal, R., Marín, B. V., & Pérez-Stable, E. J. (1987). Hispanic familism and acculturation: What changes and what doesn't? "Hispanic Journal of Behavioral Sciences, 9," 397-412.

Salmon, C. T., & Nichols, J. S. (1983). The next-birthday method of respondent selection. *Public Opinion Quarterly, 47,* 270-276.

Saltzman, S. P., Stoddard, A. M., McCusker, J., Moon, M. W., & Mayer, K. H. (1987). Reliability of self-reported sexual behavior risk factors for HIV infection in homosexual men. *Public Health Reports, 102,* 692-697.

Santisteban, D., & Szapocznik, J. (1981). Adaptation of the Multidimensional Functional Assessment Questionnaire for use with Hispanic elders. *Hispanic Journal of Behavioral Sciences, 3,* 301-308.

Schaeffer, N. C. (1980). Evaluating race-of-interviewer effects in a national survey. *Sociological Methods and Research, 8,* 400-419.

Schoua, A. S. (1985). *An English/Spanish test of decentering for the translation of questionnaires.* (Doctoral). *Dissertation Abstracts International, 46,* DA8511857.

Secherest, L., Fay, T. L., & Zaidi, S. M. H. (1972). Problems of translation in cross-cultural research. *Journal of Cross-Cultural Psychology, 3,* 41-56.

Shlifer, E., & Barrios, A. (1974). Undercounting of Spanish American clients in our reporting system. *Exchanges, 2*(5), 10-12.

Shoemaker, P. J., Reese, S. D., & Danielson, W. A. (1985). *Media in ethnic context.* Austin: University of Texas, College of Communication.

Shorkey, C. T., & Whiteman, V. L. (1978). Correlations between standard English and dialectical Spanish versions of five personality scales. *Psychological Reports, 43,* 910.

Staples, R. (1976). *Introduction to Black sociology.* New York: McGraw-Hill.

Stewart, D. W. (1984). *Secondary analysis: Information sources and methods.* Beverly Hills, CA: Sage.

Strahan, R., & Gerbasi, K. C.(1972). Short, homogeneous versions of the Marlowe-Crowne Social Desirability Scale. *Journal of Clinical Psychology, 28,* 191-193.

Szapocznik, J., & Kurtines, W. (1980). Acculturation, biculturalism, and adjustment among Cuban Americans. In A. M. Padilla (Ed.), *Acculturation: Theory, models, and some new findings* (pp. 139-159). Boulder, CO: Westview.

Szapocznik, J., Scopetta, M. A., Kurtines, W., & Aranalde, M. A. (1978). Theory and measurement of acculturation. *Interamerican Journal of Psychology/Revista Interamericana de Psicología, 12,* 113-130.

Tajfel, H., & Turner, J. (1979). An integrative theory of intergroup conflict. In W. G. Austin & S. Worchel (Eds.), *The social psychology of intergroup relations* (pp. 33-47). Belmont, CA: Brooks/Cole.

Thomas, W. I., & Znaniecki, F. (1918). *The Polish peasant in Europe and America* Vols. 1-5. Boston: R. Badger.

Tienda, M., & Ortiz, V. (1986). "Hispanicity" and the 1980 census. *Social Science Quarterly, 67,* 3-20.

Treviño, F. (1987). Standardized terminology for Hispanic populations. *American Journal of Public Health, 77,* 69-72.

Treviño, F. M. (1984). *Health indicators for Hispanics, Black and White Americans* (Vital and Health Statistics Series 10, No. 148, DHHS Publication No. (PHS) 84-1576). Hyatsville, MD: National Center for Health Statistics.

Treviño, F. M. (1985). Cross-cultural aspects. In National Center for Health Statistics (Ed.), *Plan and operation of the Hispanic Health and Nutrition Examination Survey, 1982-1984* (pp. 4-6). Washington, DC: Government Printing Office.

Triandis, H. C. (1972). *The analysis of subjective culture.* New York: John Wiley.

Triandis, H. C., Malpass, R. S., & Davidson, A. (1973). Cross-cultural psychology. *Biennial Review of Anthropology.* Palo Alto, CA: Annual Reviews.

Triandis, H. C., & Marín, G. (1983). Etic plus emic versus pseudoetic: A test of a basic assumption of contemporary cross-cultural psychology. *Journal of Cross-Cultural Psychology, 14,* 489-500.

Triandis, H. C., Marín, G., Betancourt, H., Lisansky, J., & Chang, B. (1982). *Dimensions of familism among Hispanic and mainstream Navy recruits.* Chicago: University of Illinois, Department of Psychology.

Triandis, H. C., Marín, G., Hui, C. H., Lisansky, J., & Ottati, V. (1984) Role perceptions of Hispanic young adults. *Journal of Cross-Cultural Psychology, 15,* 297-320.

Triandis, H. C., Marín, G., & Betancourt, H. (1984). Simpatía as a cultural script of Hispanics. *Journal of Personality and Social Psychology, 47,* 1363-1375.

Valle, R., & Martinez, C. (1980). Natural networks among Mexicano elderly in the United States: Implications for mental health. In M. R. Miranda & R. A. Ruiz (Eds.), *Chicano aging and mental health.* Washington, DC: Government Printing Office.

Waksberg, J. (1978). Sampling methods for random digit dialing. *Journal of the American Statistical Association, 73,* 40-46.

Warner, K. E. (1978). Possible increases in the underreporting of cigarette consumption. *Journal of the American Statistical Association, 73*, 314-318.

Weeks, M. F., & Moore, R. P. (1981). Ethnicity-of-interviewer effects on ethnic respondents. *Public Opinion Quarterly, 45*, 245-249.

Welch, S., Comer, J., & Steinman, M. (1973). Interviewing in a Mexican American community: An investigation of some potential sources of response bias. *Public Opinion Quarterly, 37*, 115-126.

Werner, O., & Campbell, D. T. (1970). Translating, working through interpreters and the problem of decentering. In R. N. & R. Cohen (Eds.), *A handbook of method in cultural anthropology*. New York: American Museum of Natural History.

Wesley, F., & Karr, C. (1966). Problems in establishing norms for cross-cultural comparisons. *International Journal of Psychology, 1*, 257-262.

Wilson, W. J. (1974). The new black sociology. Reflections on the "insiders" and "outsiders" controversy. In J. E. Blackwell & M. Janowitz (Eds.), *Black sociologists: Historical and contemporary perspectives*. Chicago: University of Chicago Press.

Yankauer, A. (1987). Hispanic/Latino—What's in a name? *American Journal of Public Health, 77*, 15-17.

Zusman, M. E., & Olson, A. O. (1977). Gathering complete responses from Mexican Americans by personal interviews. *Journal of Social Issues, 33*(4), 46-55.

Index

About the Authors

Gerardo Marín received his Ph.D. in social psychology in 1979 from DePaul University and is currently Professor of Psychology at the University of San Francisco. His primary research interests are centered on Hispanics and how culture affects behavior. He has conducted a large number of studies in interpersonal perception, prejudice, health promotion, and disease prevention. In addition he has published a number of methodological studies regarding research with ethnic minorities. He is a Fellow of the American Psychological Association and President of the Interamerican Society of Psychology (1989-1991). He has received awards for his research from the National Coalition of Hispanic Health and Human Services Organizations (COSSMHO) and from the national psychological associations of Spain and Colombia.

Barbara VanOss Marín received her doctoral training in applied social psychology from Loyola University of Chicago (1981) and carried out postdoctoral work in health psychology at the University of California, San Francisco (UCSF). She is currently Associate Adjunct Professor of Epidemiology and Biostatistics at UCSF. Current research projects include the expansion of a culturally appropriate community intervention on smoking cessation for Hispanics and an assessment of attitudes and behaviors related to AIDS prevention activities among Hispanics in various parts of the country.